Carnivore Diet

The Ultimate Guide to Healing Your Body, Losing Weight, and Boosting Energy Levels by Embracing the Ancestral Wisdom of a Carnivore Lifestyle

Amanda Quinn

Carnivore Diet
© Copyright 2024 by Amanda Quinn
All rights reserved

TABLE OF CONTENTS

Amanda Quinn

INTRODUCTION

What is the Carnivore Diet?

The Carnivore Diet is a revolutionary eating approach that has been gaining traction in recent years, captivating the attention of health enthusiasts, fitness buffs, and those seeking to optimize their overall well-being. At its core, this diet is centered around the consumption of animal-based foods, eschewing all plant-based options. Imagine a world where your plate is adorned with succulent cuts of meat, sizzling bacon, and rich, nourishing eggs—a world where the traditional notion of a balanced diet is challenged, and the focus shifts to embracing our ancestral roots.

Picture yourself as a hunter-gatherer, roaming the vast landscapes of our prehistoric past. Our ancestors thrived on a diet that was primarily composed of animal products, relying on the nutrient-dense sustenance provided by the flesh and organs of the beasts they hunted. The Carnivore Diet seeks to emulate this primal way of eating, stripping away the modern-day processed foods, sugars, and carbohydrates that have become so prevalent in our diets.

The beauty of the Carnivore Diet lies in its simplicity. By eliminating all plant-based foods, you are essentially removing the potential for dietary irritants, antinutrients, and inflammatory compounds that can wreak havoc on your digestive system and overall health. Instead, you are fueling your body with the most bioavailable and easily digestible nutrients found in animal products, such as high-quality protein, healthy fats, and essential vitamins and minerals.

Contrary to popular belief, the Carnivore Diet is not a one-size-fits-all approach. It allows for flexibility and customization based on individual needs and preferences. Some adherents choose to focus solely on beef, embracing the simplicity and nutrient density of this majestic animal. Others may incorporate a wider variety of animal products, such as pork, poultry, fish, and dairy, depending on their tolerances and goals.

The Carnivore Diet is not just about what you eat; it's about what you don't eat. By eliminating plant-based foods, you are bidding farewell to the carbohydrates, sugars, and processed junk that have become staples in modern diets. This absence of dietary stressors allows your body to focus on healing, reducing inflammation, and optimizing its functions. Many adherents report improved digestion, increased energy levels, clearer skin, and a newfound sense of vitality.

Critics may argue that the Carnivore Diet is extreme or lacking in variety, but the truth is that animal products provide a wide array of essential nutrients that our bodies crave. From the rich, satiating fats found in grass-fed beef to the immune-boosting properties of organ meats, the Carnivore Diet offers a nutrient-dense approach to nourishing your body. It challenges the notion that we need a diverse array of plant-based foods to thrive, instead focusing on the most efficient and bioavailable sources of nutrition.

Embarking on the Carnivore Diet is not just a dietary choice; it's a lifestyle shift. It requires a willingness to break free from the conventional wisdom surrounding nutrition and to embrace a new way of thinking about food. It demands a level of commitment and discipline, as you navigate a world filled with tempting carbohydrates and processed snacks. But for those who persevere, the rewards can be truly transformative.

As you delve deeper into the world of the Carnivore Diet, you'll discover a supportive community of like-minded individuals who have experienced the profound benefits of this way of eating. From online forums to local meetups, you'll find a wealth of knowledge, encouragement, and inspiration to help you along your journey.

The Carnivore Diet is not a passing fad or a quick fix; it's a return to our ancestral roots, a celebration of the nourishing power of animal foods, and a path to optimal health and vitality. So, as you embark on this transformative journey, remember to listen to your body, trust the process, and embrace the primal wisdom that has sustained our species for millennia. Welcome to the world of the Carnivore Diet, where simplicity meets nourishment, and where your health takes center stage.

The Ancestral Roots of the Carnivore Diet

The carnivore diet, a way of eating that focuses solely on animal products, may seem like a modern trend, but its roots can be traced back to our ancestral past. For millions of years, our early human ancestors relied heavily on meat for their survival, as it provided them with the necessary nutrients, energy, and fat to thrive in harsh environments.

The diet of early humans, particularly during the Paleolithic era, consisted primarily of animals hunted for their meat, organs, and marrow. This way of eating allowed our ancestors to adapt to various climates and landscapes, from the savannas of Africa to the frigid tundras of the Ice Age.

The importance of meat in the human diet is evident in the evolution of our physiology. Our digestive system, including our stomach acid and bile production, is optimized for breaking down and absorbing nutrients from animal products. Additionally, our teeth and jaw structure are designed for tearing and chewing meat, further highlighting our evolutionary adaptation to a carnivorous diet.

The reliance on animal products for survival is not unique to early humans. Many indigenous cultures around the world, such as the Inuit of the Arctic and the Maasai of East Africa, have traditionally thrived on diets consisting almost entirely of meat, fish, and animal fat. These cultures demonstrate the potential for humans to maintain excellent health and physical performance on a carnivore diet.

The shift away from a meat-based diet began with the advent of agriculture around 10,000 years ago. As humans started cultivating crops and domesticating animals, their diets became increasingly diverse, incorporating more plant-based foods. While this change allowed for the growth of civilizations and population expansion, it also marked a departure from the way our ancestors had eaten for millions of years.

In recent years, the carnivore diet has gained popularity as a way to reconnect with our ancestral roots and optimize health. Proponents of the diet argue that by eliminating plant-based foods and focusing solely on animal products, we can better align our eating habits with our evolutionary past and improve various aspects of our well-being.

The carnivore diet's emphasis on nutrient-dense animal products, such as organ meats, fatty cuts of meat, and fish, mirrors the eating habits of our ancestors who prized these foods for their life-sustaining properties. By consuming a wide variety of animal products, followers of the carnivore diet aim to obtain all the essential nutrients needed for optimal health, without the need for plant-based foods.

While the carnivore diet remains controversial and more research is needed to fully understand its long-term effects, its ancestral roots provide a compelling argument for its potential benefits. By embracing the wisdom of our ancestors and reconnecting with our evolutionary past, the carnivore diet offers a unique approach to nourishing our bodies and optimizing our health in the modern world.

Why the Carnivore Diet is Gaining Popularity

The carnivore diet, a dietary approach that emphasizes consuming only animal products and eliminates all plant-based foods, has been gaining traction in recent years. This unconventional way of eating has attracted a growing number of followers who claim it has improved their health, energy levels, and overall well-being. The diet's proponents argue that by focusing on nutrient-dense animal foods and eliminating potentially problematic plant compounds, followers can optimize their health and reduce the risk of chronic diseases.

One of the main reasons the carnivore diet has gained popularity is its simplicity. Unlike many other diets that require strict calorie counting, macronutrient tracking, or portion control, the carnivore diet has just one rule: eat only animal products. This straightforward approach appeals to those who find complex dietary guidelines overwhelming or difficult to follow. By eliminating the need to plan and prepare a variety of meals, the carnivore diet can make mealtime less stressful and more manageable for some individuals.

Another factor contributing to the diet's growing popularity is the reported health benefits experienced by many of its followers. Anecdotal evidence suggests that the carnivore diet may help with weight loss, improved digestion, reduced inflammation, and better mental clarity. Some adherents claim that the diet has helped them resolve chronic health issues, such as autoimmune disorders, digestive problems, and skin conditions. While more research is needed to substantiate these claims, the positive experiences shared by carnivore diet followers have sparked curiosity and interest among those seeking alternative approaches to health and wellness.

The carnivore diet's emphasis on high-quality animal products, such as grass-fed beef, pasture-raised eggs, and wild-caught fish, aligns with the growing interest in ancestral health and the belief that our bodies are best adapted to the diets of our hunter-gatherer ancestors. Proponents argue that the modern Western diet, characterized by processed foods, refined carbohydrates, and industrial seed oils, is a major contributor to the rise of chronic diseases. By eliminating these potentially harmful foods and focusing on nutrient-dense animal products, carnivore diet followers believe they are providing their bodies with the fuel they need to thrive.

The rise of the carnivore diet can also be attributed to the influence of high-profile advocates and success stories shared on social media. Well-known figures in the health and fitness industry, such as Dr. Shawn Baker and Jordan Peterson, have publicly embraced the carnivore diet and shared their experiences with their large followings. Their stories of improved health, increased energy, and weight loss have inspired others to try the diet for themselves. Additionally, the growing number of online communities dedicated to the carnivore diet has created a supportive network for those interested in learning more about the approach and connecting with like-minded individuals.

Despite its growing popularity, the carnivore diet remains controversial, and many health professionals express concerns about its long-term safety and sustainability. Critics argue that eliminating entire food groups, such as fruits, vegetables, and whole grains, can lead to nutrient deficiencies and potentially increase the risk of certain chronic diseases. They also point out that the diet's high saturated fat content may raise cholesterol levels and increase the risk of heart disease in some individuals.

Furthermore, the lack of scientific research specifically examining the long-term effects of the carnivore diet makes it difficult to draw definitive conclusions about its safety and efficacy.

Common Misconceptions About the Carnivore Diet

The carnivore diet has gained popularity in recent years, with proponents claiming that consuming only animal products can lead to improved health, weight loss, and increased energy levels. However, this unconventional approach to nutrition has also given rise to numerous misconceptions and concerns. In this chapter, we will address some of the most common misconceptions surrounding the carnivore diet, providing evidence-based information to help readers make informed decisions about their dietary choices.

One of the most prevalent misconceptions about the carnivore diet is that it is inherently unhealthy due to its high saturated fat content. While it is true that animal products, particularly red meat, contain saturated fats, recent research has called into question the long-held belief that saturated fats are the primary culprit behind heart disease and other health issues. A comprehensive review published in the Annals of Internal Medicine found no significant evidence linking saturated fat consumption to an increased risk of heart disease, stroke, or type 2 diabetes. Furthermore, the carnivore diet typically includes a variety of animal products, such as fatty fish and organ meats, which are rich in essential nutrients like omega-3 fatty acids and vitamins A and B12.

Another common misconception is that the carnivore diet lacks fiber, which is essential for maintaining a healthy digestive system. While it is true that plant-based foods are the primary sources of dietary fiber, proponents of the carnivore diet argue that the need for fiber is greatly reduced when consuming only animal products. They claim that the absence of plant-based foods, which can be difficult to digest and may cause inflammation in some individuals, allows the gut to heal and function more efficiently. Additionally, some animal products, such as collagen-rich bone broth, may help support gut health by promoting the growth of beneficial bacteria and reducing inflammation.

Critics of the carnivore diet often express concern about the potential for nutrient deficiencies, particularly in vitamins and minerals typically found in plant-based foods. However, a well-planned carnivore diet can provide a wide array of essential nutrients. For example, beef liver is an excellent source of vitamin A, while fatty fish like salmon and sardines are rich in vitamin D and omega-3 fatty acids. Eggs and dairy products, if included in the diet, can provide additional nutrients such as vitamin K2 and calcium. While it may be more challenging to obtain certain nutrients, such as vitamin C, on a carnivore diet, some proponents argue that the body's need for these nutrients may be lower in the absence of carbohydrates and plant-based toxins.

A fourth misconception surrounding the carnivore diet is that it is unsustainable and environmentally irresponsible. While it is true that industrial animal agriculture can have negative environmental impacts, it is essential to consider the source and production methods of the animal products consumed. Proponents of the carnivore diet often advocate for consuming grass-fed, pasture-raised, and organically produced animal products, which can have a lower environmental impact compared to conventionally raised animals. Additionally, some argue that the use of regenerative agricultural practices, such as rotational grazing, can actually help to improve soil health and sequester carbon.

Who Can Benefit from the Carnivore Diet?

The carnivore diet, with its focus on consuming only animal products, may seem like an extreme approach to nutrition. However, many individuals have found significant benefits from adopting this way of eating. While the carnivore diet may not be suitable for everyone, certain groups of people may find it particularly beneficial for their health and well-being.

One group that may benefit from the carnivore diet is those struggling with chronic digestive issues, such as irritable bowel syndrome (IBS), inflammatory bowel disease (IBD), or leaky gut syndrome. By eliminating plant-based foods, which can be difficult to digest and may trigger symptoms, the carnivore diet can help alleviate digestive discomfort and promote gut healing. The high-quality protein and nutrient-dense animal products consumed on this diet can also support the repair and regeneration of the gut lining.

Individuals with autoimmune conditions may also find relief through the carnivore diet. Autoimmune diseases occur when the body's immune system mistakenly attacks its own tissues, leading to inflammation and various symptoms. The carnivore diet removes many common dietary triggers, such as gluten, lectins, and other plant compounds that can exacerbate autoimmune reactions. By reducing inflammation and allowing the body to focus on healing, the carnivore diet may help manage symptoms and improve overall quality of life for those with autoimmune conditions.

Another group that may benefit from the carnivore diet is people seeking to lose weight and improve body composition. The high protein content of the carnivore diet can help preserve lean muscle mass while promoting fat loss, leading to a more favorable body composition. Additionally, the absence of carbohydrates and the satiating nature of protein and fat can naturally reduce appetite and calorie intake, making it easier to achieve and maintain a healthy weight.

Athletes and fitness enthusiasts may also find the carnivore diet advantageous for optimizing performance and recovery. The high-quality protein from animal sources provides the essential amino acids necessary for muscle repair and growth, while the fat content supports hormone production and energy levels. By minimizing inflammation and supporting overall health, the carnivore diet can help athletes perform at their best and recover more efficiently from intense training sessions.

Individuals with neurological conditions, such as epilepsy or Alzheimer's disease, may also benefit from the carnivore diet. The high-fat content of the diet can promote the production of ketones, which serve as an alternative fuel source for the brain. This metabolic shift has been shown to have neuroprotective effects and may improve cognitive function, reduce seizure frequency, and slow the progression of neurodegenerative diseases.

CHAPTER 1

THE SCIENCE BEHIND THE CARNIVORE DIET

The Role of Nutrients in an All-Meat Diet

In the realm of the Carnivore Diet, nutrients play a paramount role in ensuring optimal health and well-being. When embarking on an all-meat diet, it is crucial to understand the unique nutritional profile of animal-based foods and how they contribute to the proper functioning of our bodies. Many people are surprised to learn that an all-meat diet can provide a comprehensive array of essential nutrients, challenging the conventional wisdom that a varied diet is necessary for optimal nutrition.

At the heart of the Carnivore Diet lies the concept of nutrient density. Animal products, particularly those from well-raised and properly sourced animals, are among the most nutrient-dense foods on the planet. They offer an unparalleled concentration of essential vitamins, minerals, and other vital compounds that our bodies require to thrive. By focusing on these nutrient-rich foods, the Carnivore Diet ensures that our bodies receive the nourishment they need to function at their best.

One of the most significant nutrients in an all-meat diet is protein. High-quality animal protein is the building block of our muscles, bones, and tissues, and it plays a crucial role in repair, growth, and maintenance. Unlike plant-based proteins, animal proteins are considered "complete," meaning they contain all the essential amino acids our bodies need in the right proportions. This makes animal protein more bioavailable and efficiently utilized by our bodies, promoting optimal health and performance.

Fat is another essential nutrient that takes center stage in the Carnivore Diet. Contrary to popular belief, dietary fat is not the enemy. In fact, healthy fats from animal sources are vital for hormone production, brain function, and cell membrane integrity. Saturated fats, often demonized in mainstream nutrition, are actually essential for the absorption of fat-soluble vitamins and play a crucial role in maintaining optimal health. The Carnivore Diet embraces the consumption of healthy animal fats, such as those found in grass-fed beef, wild-caught fish, and pasture-raised eggs.

Vitamins and minerals are also abundant in an all-meat diet. Animal products are rich in bioavailable forms of essential vitamins and minerals, such as vitamin B12, iron, zinc, and selenium. These nutrients are crucial for various bodily functions, including energy production, immune function, and cognitive health. By consuming a variety of animal products, including organ meats, the Carnivore Diet ensures that our bodies receive a comprehensive array of these vital micronutrients.

One of the unique aspects of the Carnivore Diet is the emphasis on organ meats. Often overlooked in modern diets, organ meats are true nutritional powerhouses. They are packed with essential nutrients that are difficult to obtain from muscle meat alone. For example, liver is an exceptional source of vitamin A, copper, and folate, while heart is rich in CoQ10, a powerful antioxidant. Incorporating organ meats into your Carnivore Diet can significantly boost your nutrient intake and support optimal health.

It's important to note that the quality of the animal products you consume matters greatly. Choosing grass-fed, pasture-raised, and wild-caught options ensures that you are getting the most nutrient-dense and ethically sourced foods possible. These animals are raised in their natural environments, consuming their native diets, which leads to a superior nutritional profile compared to conventionally raised animals.

When following the Carnivore Diet, it's essential to listen to your body and pay attention to how you feel. Everyone's nutritional needs are unique, and what works for one person may not work for another. Some individuals may thrive on a diet composed primarily of beef, while others may require a more varied approach, incorporating other animal products like pork, poultry, and fish. The key is to experiment, monitor your body's responses, and adjust your diet accordingly.

Critics of the Carnivore Diet often argue that it lacks dietary fiber, which is typically obtained from plant-based sources. However, many proponents of the diet report improved digestion and bowel function, suggesting that dietary fiber may not be as essential as once thought. The absence of plant-based irritants and antinutrients may allow the digestive system to function more efficiently, even without the presence of fiber.

As you embark on your Carnivore Diet journey, it's crucial to educate yourself about the nutrients found in animal products and how they contribute to your overall health. Seek out high-quality sources of meat, prioritize nutrient-dense options like organ meats, and listen to your body's feedback. By focusing on the nutrient density of an all-meat diet, you can unlock the potential for optimal health, vitality, and well-being.

How the Carnivore Diet Affects Gut Health

The carnivore diet, which consists solely of animal products, has gained attention for its potential impact on various aspects of health, including gut health. The human gut is a complex ecosystem, home to trillions of microorganisms that play a crucial role in digestion, immunity, and overall well-being. By eliminating plant-based foods and focusing on nutrient-dense animal products, the carnivore diet can significantly influence the gut microbiome and digestive function.

One of the primary ways the carnivore diet affects gut health is by reducing the intake of fermentable carbohydrates, such as fiber and resistant starch, which are commonly found in plant-based foods. These carbohydrates are often poorly absorbed in the small intestine and can lead to digestive discomfort, bloating, and gas when they reach the large intestine and are fermented by gut bacteria. By minimizing the consumption of these fermentable carbohydrates, the carnivore diet may help alleviate digestive issues and promote a more comfortable gut experience for some individuals.

Moreover, the carnivore diet's emphasis on high-quality animal protein and fat can support the integrity of the gut lining. Collagen, which is abundant in connective tissues found in animal products like bone broth and organ meats, plays a vital role in maintaining the structure and function of the intestinal wall. By consuming collagen-rich foods, followers of the carnivore diet may help strengthen the gut barrier, reducing the risk of leaky gut syndrome and associated inflammatory conditions.

The carnivore diet may also benefit gut health by eliminating common irritants and allergens found in plant-based foods. Many people experience digestive distress, inflammation, and autoimmune reactions in response to substances like gluten, lectins, and phytates, which are present in grains, legumes, and certain vegetables. By removing these potential triggers, the carnivore diet can provide relief for those with food sensitivities and promote a more balanced and resilient gut environment.

However, it is essential to acknowledge that the long-term effects of the carnivore diet on gut health are not yet fully understood. Some experts argue that the lack of dietary fiber and plant-based nutrients may negatively impact the diversity and composition of the gut microbiome. A diverse gut microbiome is generally associated with better overall health, as it helps maintain a balanced immune system, regulates metabolism, and supports nutrient absorption.

To mitigate potential drawbacks and optimize gut health on the carnivore diet, it is crucial to focus on consuming a wide variety of high-quality animal products, including organ meats, bone broth, and fermented foods like kefir and yogurt. These nutrient-dense foods provide essential vitamins, minerals, and beneficial compounds that support gut function and microbial balance.

Additionally, incorporating strategies to manage stress, prioritize sleep, and engage in regular physical activity can further support gut health while following the carnivore diet. These lifestyle factors play a significant role in maintaining a healthy gut-brain axis and promoting overall digestive well-being.

As with any dietary approach, individual responses to the carnivore diet may vary. Some people may experience improvements in gut health, while others may find the lack of plant-based foods challenging or even detrimental. It is essential to listen to your body, monitor your symptoms, and work with a qualified healthcare professional to determine if the carnivore diet is the right choice for your unique needs and goals.

The Carnivore Diet and Inflammation

The carnivore diet has gained attention for its potential role in reducing inflammation, a key factor in the development of many chronic diseases. Inflammation is a natural response of the body's immune system to injury, infection, or irritation. However, when inflammation becomes chronic, it can contribute to a wide range of health problems, including heart disease, diabetes, autoimmune disorders, and certain types of cancer. By eliminating potentially inflammatory foods and focusing on nutrient-dense animal products, proponents of the carnivore diet believe it can help reduce inflammation and improve overall health.

One of the primary ways the carnivore diet may reduce inflammation is by eliminating common dietary triggers. Many plant-based foods, such as grains, legumes, and nightshade vegetables, contain compounds that can cause inflammation in some individuals. For example, lectins, found in many plant foods, are known to disrupt the gut lining and activate the immune system, leading to inflammation. By removing these foods from the diet, carnivore diet followers may experience a reduction in inflammation and associated symptoms, such as joint pain, skin issues, and digestive discomfort.

The carnivore diet's emphasis on high-quality animal products may also contribute to its anti-inflammatory effects. Grass-fed beef, for instance, contains higher levels of omega-3 fatty acids compared to grain-fed beef. Omega-3 fatty acids are known for their anti-inflammatory properties and have been shown to help reduce the risk of chronic diseases. Additionally, grass-fed beef is a rich source of conjugated linoleic acid (CLA), a type of fat that has been linked to reduced inflammation and improved immune function. By incorporating these nutrient-dense animal foods into the diet, carnivore diet followers may be able to support their body's natural anti-inflammatory processes.

Another potential mechanism by which the carnivore diet may reduce inflammation is through its impact on gut health. The gut plays a crucial role in immune function and inflammation, and an imbalance in gut bacteria, known as dysbiosis, can contribute to chronic inflammation. By eliminating many of the foods that can disrupt gut health, such as processed foods, refined carbohydrates, and industrial seed oils, the carnivore diet may help restore a healthy gut microbiome. This, in turn, can help reduce inflammation and improve overall health.

While anecdotal evidence suggests that the carnivore diet may be effective in reducing inflammation for some individuals, it is important to note that the scientific research on this topic is limited. More studies are needed to fully understand the mechanisms by which the carnivore diet may impact inflammation and to determine its long-term safety and efficacy. Additionally, the elimination of entire food groups, such as fruits and vegetables, may lead to nutrient deficiencies and other potential health risks, which should be carefully considered before adopting the diet.

It is also worth noting that the carnivore diet's potential anti-inflammatory effects may not be suitable for everyone. Some individuals may have specific health conditions or dietary needs that make the carnivore diet inappropriate or even harmful. For example, those with a history of kidney disease or gout may need to limit their intake of high-purine animal foods, which can exacerbate these conditions. As with any significant dietary change, it is essential to consult with a healthcare professional before starting the carnivore diet to assess its appropriateness for your individual needs and health status.

The Impact of the Carnivore Diet on Weight Loss

The carnivore diet has gained significant attention in recent years as a potential tool for weight loss. This unconventional approach to nutrition, which involves consuming only animal products and eliminating all plant-based foods, has been reported to lead to rapid and substantial weight loss in many adherents. However, it is essential to understand the mechanisms behind this weight loss and to consider both the potential benefits and drawbacks of adopting such a restrictive dietary plan.

One of the primary reasons the carnivore diet may lead to weight loss is its inherent ability to reduce overall calorie intake. By eliminating entire food groups, particularly carbohydrate-rich foods like grains, fruits, and vegetables, individuals following the carnivore diet often experience a significant reduction in their daily calorie consumption. This calorie deficit, combined with the satiating effects of high-protein and high-fat meals, can result in decreased hunger and a subsequent decrease in body weight.

The carnivore diet's emphasis on consuming high-quality, nutrient-dense animal products may also contribute to its weight loss potential. When individuals focus on consuming whole, minimally processed foods like grass-fed beef, wild-caught fish, and pasture-raised eggs, they are more likely to feel satisfied and nourished, reducing the likelihood of overeating or snacking on empty calories. Additionally, the high protein content of animal products can help to preserve lean muscle mass during weight loss, which is essential for maintaining a healthy metabolism and preventing the dreaded "yo-yo" effect often associated with crash diets.

Another factor that may contribute to weight loss on the carnivore diet is the reduction of inflammation in the body. Many proponents of the diet argue that eliminating plant-based foods, which can contain antinutrients and inflammatory compounds, allows the body to heal and function more efficiently. This reduction in inflammation may lead to improved insulin sensitivity, better hormonal regulation, and a more favorable body composition over time.

It is important to note, however, that the rapid weight loss often experienced in the initial stages of the carnivore diet may be largely due to water weight loss. When individuals drastically reduce their carbohydrate intake, the body begins to deplete its stored glycogen, which is accompanied by a significant loss of water. This initial water weight loss can be motivating for many people, but it is essential to recognize that sustainable, long-term weight loss requires a more gradual approach and a focus on overall body composition rather than just the number on the scale.

While the carnivore diet may lead to weight loss for some individuals, it is not without its potential drawbacks and risks. The highly restrictive nature of the diet can make it difficult to sustain long-term, and the elimination of entire food groups may increase the risk of nutrient deficiencies if not carefully planned and monitored. It is crucial for individuals considering the carnivore diet to work closely with a qualified healthcare professional to ensure they are meeting their nutritional needs and to address any potential health concerns.

Additionally, the long-term effects of the carnivore diet on weight loss and overall health are not yet well understood. While some anecdotal reports and small-scale studies suggest positive outcomes, more research is needed to fully comprehend the implications of this dietary approach. It is essential for individuals to carefully weigh the potential benefits against the risks and to consider their unique health status, goals, and preferences before embarking on such a restrictive eating plan.

The Carnivore Diet and Brain Function

The intricate relationship between diet and brain function has been the subject of numerous studies, and the carnivore diet has emerged as a fascinating approach to optimizing cognitive performance. By focusing on nutrient-dense animal products and eliminating potentially harmful plant compounds, the carnivore diet may offer unique benefits for brain health and mental well-being.

One of the key ways in which the carnivore diet supports brain function is through its high-fat content. The brain is composed of approximately 60% fat, and it relies on healthy fats for proper structure and function. The carnivore diet provides an abundance of saturated and monounsaturated fats from animal sources, such as grass-fed beef, fatty fish, and organ meats. These fats are essential for maintaining the integrity of brain cell membranes, which are crucial for effective communication between neurons.

Moreover, the high-fat nature of the carnivore diet promotes the production of ketones, which serve as an alternative fuel source for the brain. When the body is in a state of ketosis, it efficiently converts fats into ketones, which can cross the blood-brain barrier and provide energy to brain cells. This metabolic shift has been shown to have neuroprotective effects, reducing inflammation and oxidative stress in the brain. Studies have suggested that a ketogenic state may improve cognitive function, enhance memory, and even alleviate symptoms of neurological conditions such as epilepsy and Alzheimer's disease.

In addition to healthy fats, the carnivore diet provides an abundance of high-quality protein, which is essential for neurotransmitter production and brain function. Amino acids, the building blocks of protein, are required for the synthesis of neurotransmitters such as serotonin, dopamine, and GABA. These neurotransmitters play crucial roles in mood regulation, focus, and overall mental well-being. By consuming a wide variety of animal products, including organ meats, the carnivore diet ensures an optimal supply of essential amino acids to support neurotransmitter balance and brain health.

The carnivore diet also eliminates many plant compounds that can have negative effects on brain function. For example, gluten, a protein found in wheat and other grains, has been linked to neurological disorders such as gluten ataxia and peripheral neuropathy. By removing gluten and other potentially harmful plant compounds, the carnivore diet may help alleviate symptoms and promote optimal brain function in susceptible individuals.

Furthermore, the carnivore diet's emphasis on nutrient density ensures an ample supply of essential vitamins and minerals that support brain health. For instance, vitamin B12, which is found almost exclusively in animal products, is crucial for maintaining the myelin sheath that surrounds and protects nerve fibers. A deficiency in vitamin B12 can lead to neurological symptoms such as memory loss, confusion, and even dementia. The carnivore diet provides a reliable source of vitamin B12, as well as other brain-supportive nutrients like iron, zinc, and omega-3 fatty acids.

The elimination of processed foods and added sugars on the carnivore diet may also have positive effects on brain function. A diet high in refined carbohydrates and sugar has been linked to inflammation, insulin resistance, and oxidative stress, all of which can have detrimental effects on brain health. By focusing on whole, unprocessed animal foods, the carnivore diet minimizes exposure to these harmful substances and promotes a more stable blood sugar balance, which is essential for optimal brain function.

The Potential Benefits of the Carnivore Diet for Autoimmune Conditions

The Carnivore Diet has emerged as a beacon of hope for individuals struggling with autoimmune conditions, offering a potential path to remission and improved quality of life. Autoimmune disorders, such as rheumatoid arthritis, lupus, and multiple sclerosis, occur when the body's immune system mistakenly attacks its own tissues, leading to chronic inflammation, pain, and a host of debilitating symptoms. Conventional treatments often involve immunosuppressive drugs, which can have significant side effects and fail to address the root cause of the problem. This is where the Carnivore Diet comes in, providing a novel approach to managing autoimmune conditions through dietary intervention.

At its core, the Carnivore Diet is an elimination diet that removes all potential dietary triggers and focuses solely on nutrient-dense animal products. By eliminating plant-based foods, including grains, legumes, and even fruits and vegetables, the Carnivore Diet aims to reduce the intake of antinutrients, such as lectins and phytates, which can contribute to intestinal permeability and immune system dysfunction. When the gut lining becomes compromised, it allows partially digested food particles and toxins to enter the bloodstream, triggering an immune response and perpetuating the cycle of inflammation.

One of the key benefits of the Carnivore Diet for autoimmune conditions lies in its ability to promote gut healing. By removing irritants and focusing on easily digestible animal products, the diet allows the gut lining to repair itself, reducing intestinal permeability and calming the overactive immune system. Many individuals with autoimmune conditions report significant improvements in their symptoms, including reduced pain, increased energy levels, and better overall well-being, after adopting a Carnivore Diet.

The nutrient density of animal products also plays a crucial role in supporting immune system function and reducing inflammation. High-quality animal protein provides the building blocks for immune cells and helps regulate the immune response. Healthy fats, such as those found in grass-fed beef and wild-caught fish, are rich in anti-inflammatory omega-3 fatty acids, which can help counteract the chronic inflammation associated with autoimmune disorders. Vitamins and minerals, such as vitamin D, zinc, and selenium, are also abundant in animal products and are essential for proper immune system function.

Another potential benefit of the Carnivore Diet for autoimmune conditions is its ability to reduce oxidative stress. Oxidative stress occurs when there is an imbalance between the production of free radicals and the body's ability to neutralize them, leading to cellular damage and inflammation. Animal products, particularly organ meats, are rich in antioxidants like glutathione and CoQ10, which help combat oxidative stress and protect against cellular damage. By reducing oxidative stress, the Carnivore Diet may help alleviate the burden on the immune system and promote healing.

It's important to note that the Carnivore Diet is not a one-size-fits-all solution for autoimmune conditions. While many individuals have experienced remarkable improvements, others may require additional interventions or modifications to the diet. Some people may benefit from a more gradual transition, starting with an elimination diet that removes common triggers like gluten, dairy, and soy, before progressing to a full Carnivore Diet. Others may need to incorporate specific nutrient-dense foods, such as organ meats or bone broth, to support their unique nutritional needs.

As with any dietary intervention, it's crucial to work with a qualified healthcare practitioner who can provide personalized guidance and monitor your progress. Autoimmune conditions can be complex, and it's essential to have professional support to ensure that your nutritional needs are met and any potential concerns are addressed. Regular check-ins and monitoring of biomarkers can help track your progress and make necessary adjustments along the way.

While the Carnivore Diet holds great promise for managing autoimmune conditions, it's important to approach it with realistic expectations and a commitment to self-experimentation. Every individual's journey is unique, and what works for one person may not work for another. It's essential to listen to your body, pay attention to your symptoms, and make adjustments as needed. Some people may experience an initial worsening of symptoms, known as the "autoimmune flare," as their bodies adapt to the new diet. This is often temporary and can be managed with the guidance of a healthcare practitioner.

In addition to dietary changes, incorporating lifestyle factors that support immune system function and reduce stress can further enhance the benefits of the Carnivore Diet for autoimmune conditions. Adequate sleep, regular exercise, stress management techniques, and exposure to natural light can all contribute to a more balanced and resilient immune system. Creating a holistic approach that encompasses both diet and lifestyle factors can provide a solid foundation for managing autoimmune conditions and promoting overall health and well-being.

As the research on the Carnivore Diet and autoimmune conditions continues to evolve, it's essential to stay informed and open-minded. While anecdotal evidence and personal success stories are compelling, more rigorous scientific studies are needed to fully understand the mechanisms behind the diet's potential benefits. As always, it's crucial to approach any dietary change with caution and under the guidance of a qualified healthcare professional.

For individuals with autoimmune conditions who have struggled to find relief through conventional treatments, the Carnivore Diet offers a glimmer of hope. By removing potential triggers, promoting gut healing, and providing a nutrient-dense approach to nourishment, this unconventional way of eating may hold the key to improved symptoms, increased quality of life, and a renewed sense of vitality. With dedication, self-experimentation, and professional guidance, the Carnivore Diet can be a powerful tool in the arsenal against autoimmune disorders, empowering individuals to take control of their health and reclaim their lives.

Debunking Myths About the Carnivore Diet and Health

The carnivore diet, which involves consuming only animal products, has been the subject of much debate and speculation in the health and nutrition world. As with any unconventional dietary approach, numerous myths and misconceptions have emerged, leading to confusion and skepticism among those considering adopting this way of eating. In this chapter, we will explore and debunk some of the most common myths surrounding the carnivore diet and its impact on health.

Myth #1: The carnivore diet lacks essential nutrients

One of the most prevalent myths about the carnivore diet is that it is nutritionally incomplete and lacks essential vitamins and minerals. However, this belief fails to recognize the nutrient density of animal products. Meat, especially organ meats, is rich in bioavailable vitamins and minerals, such as vitamin B12, iron, zinc, and selenium. Additionally, fatty fish and egg yolks provide valuable omega-3 fatty acids and fat-soluble vitamins like vitamin A and D. By consuming a variety of high-quality animal products, followers of the carnivore diet can obtain all the essential nutrients needed for optimal health.

Myth #2: The carnivore diet causes cardiovascular disease

Another common myth is that the high saturated fat content of the carnivore diet leads to an increased risk of cardiovascular disease. This belief stems from the long-standing demonization of saturated fat in the mainstream health community. However, recent research has challenged this notion, suggesting that saturated fat from natural, whole-food sources may not be as harmful as previously thought. In fact, some studies have found that diets high in saturated fat from animal products can improve cardiovascular risk factors, such as increasing HDL (good) cholesterol and reducing triglycerides.

Myth #3: The carnivore diet leads to constipation and digestive issues

Many people assume that the absence of fiber in the carnivore diet will inevitably lead to constipation and other digestive problems. While fiber is often touted as essential for regular bowel movements, this is not the case for everyone. The carnivore diet's focus on easily digestible animal products can actually alleviate digestive distress for many individuals, particularly those with sensitivities to plant-based foods. The elimination of fermentable carbohydrates and potential irritants found in plants can promote a more comfortable and efficient digestive process.

Myth #4: The carnivore diet is unsustainable and harmful to the environment

Critics of the carnivore diet often argue that it is unsustainable and contributes to environmental degradation due to the perceived high carbon footprint of animal agriculture. However, this myth fails to consider the potential benefits of regenerative and sustainable farming practices. When animals are raised in harmony with their natural environment, such as through rotational grazing and pasture-based systems, they can actually help restore soil health, sequester carbon, and promote biodiversity. By supporting local, ethical, and sustainably-raised animal products, followers of the carnivore diet can contribute to a more resilient and environmentally-friendly food system.

Myth #5: The carnivore diet is a fad and not backed by science

Finally, some people dismiss the carnivore diet as a passing fad without any scientific basis. While it is true that long-term studies on the carnivore diet are limited, there is a growing body of anecdotal evidence and short-term research suggesting its potential benefits for various health conditions, such as improving insulin sensitivity, reducing inflammation, and promoting weight loss. Additionally, the carnivore diet's emphasis on nutrient-dense, whole-food animal products aligns with the ancestral eating patterns that have sustained human health for millions of years.

The Carnivore Diet and Athletic Performance

The carnivore diet, with its emphasis on high-quality animal products and elimination of plant-based foods, has gained popularity among athletes and fitness enthusiasts seeking to optimize their performance. Proponents of the diet claim that it can provide numerous benefits for athletic pursuits, including increased strength, improved endurance, and faster recovery times. By focusing on nutrient-dense animal foods and reducing potential sources of inflammation, the carnivore diet may offer a unique approach to fueling athletic performance.

One of the primary ways the carnivore diet can support athletic performance is through its high protein content. Animal products, such as meat, eggs, and fish, are rich sources of complete proteins, containing all the essential amino acids necessary for muscle growth and repair. Adequate protein intake is crucial for athletes, as it helps support the development and maintenance of lean body mass, which is essential for strength and power. By consuming a diet rich in high-quality animal proteins, carnivore diet followers may be able to optimize their muscle-building potential and enhance their overall athletic performance.

The carnivore diet's potential to reduce inflammation may also contribute to improved athletic performance. Inflammation is a natural response to intense physical activity, but chronic inflammation can hinder recovery and impair performance. By eliminating potentially inflammatory plant foods, such as grains, legumes, and processed oils, the carnivore diet may help reduce systemic inflammation and promote faster recovery between training sessions. This can allow athletes to maintain a more consistent and intense training schedule, ultimately leading to improved performance outcomes.

Another potential benefit of the carnivore diet for athletes is its impact on body composition. The high protein and fat content of the diet can help support the maintenance of lean body mass while promoting fat loss. This is particularly important for athletes who need to maintain a specific weight or body composition for their sport. By focusing on nutrient-dense animal foods and eliminating processed carbohydrates, the carnivore diet may help athletes achieve and maintain an optimal body composition for their specific athletic goals.

The simplicity of the carnivore diet can also be advantageous for athletes with busy schedules or limited time for meal preparation. By eliminating the need to plan and prepare a wide variety of foods, the carnivore diet can make mealtime more manageable and less stressful. This can be particularly beneficial for athletes who are balancing training, competition, and other life commitments. The straightforward nature of the diet allows athletes to focus on consuming high-quality animal products without the added complexity of incorporating a diverse range of plant-based foods.

While the carnivore diet may offer potential benefits for athletic performance, it is important to consider the individual needs and goals of each athlete. Some athletes may require a higher carbohydrate intake to support their specific training demands, while others may benefit from the inclusion of certain plant-based foods for their unique nutritional properties. It is essential for athletes considering the carnivore diet to work closely with a sports nutritionist or healthcare professional to ensure that their dietary approach is tailored to their specific needs and goals.

It is also worth noting that the long-term safety and efficacy of the carnivore diet for athletic performance have not been extensively studied. More research is needed to fully understand the impact of the diet on various aspects of athletic performance, including strength, endurance, and recovery. Athletes should be aware of the potential risks associated with eliminating entire food groups, such as nutrient deficiencies and digestive issues, and should monitor their health closely when adopting the carnivore diet.

CHAPTER 2

GETTING STARTED WITH THE CARNIVORE DIET

Preparing Mentally and Physically for the Carnivore Diet

Embarking on a carnivore diet requires a significant shift in both mindset and lifestyle. This unconventional approach to nutrition, which involves consuming only animal products and eliminating all plant-based foods, can be challenging for many individuals who are accustomed to a more varied diet. To ensure a smooth transition and increase the likelihood of long-term success, it is essential to prepare both mentally and physically before diving into the world of carnivory.

One of the most crucial aspects of mental preparation is setting clear and realistic goals. Take the time to reflect on your reasons for wanting to try the carnivore diet, whether it be for weight loss, improved health, or increased energy levels. Write down your goals and create a plan of action that outlines the steps you will take to achieve them. Remember that progress may be slow and steady, and it is important to celebrate small victories along the way.

Another key component of mental preparation is educating yourself about the carnivore diet and its potential benefits and risks. Read books, articles, and testimonials from individuals who have successfully adopted this way of eating. Engage with online communities and forums to learn from the experiences of others and to find support and encouragement. The more knowledge you have about the carnivore diet, the more confident and prepared you will feel as you begin your journey.

It is also essential to prepare yourself for the potential challenges and obstacles that may arise during your transition to the carnivore diet. Many people experience a period of adjustment known as the "adaptation phase," which can include symptoms such as fatigue, headaches, and digestive discomfort. Knowing that these symptoms are temporary and are a normal part of the body's adjustment to a new way of eating can help you stay motivated and committed to your goals.

In addition to mental preparation, it is crucial to ensure that you are physically ready to embark on the carnivore diet. This means taking the time to stock your kitchen with high-quality, nutrient-dense animal products such as grass-fed beef, wild-caught fish, and pasture-raised eggs. Invest in a good quality meat thermometer to ensure that you are cooking your proteins to the appropriate temperature, and consider purchasing a slow cooker or pressure cooker to make meal preparation more efficient.

It is also important to prioritize hydration when preparing for the carnivore diet. As you eliminate plant-based foods, which can be a significant source of dietary water, it becomes even more crucial to ensure that you are drinking enough fluids throughout the day. Aim to consume at least half your body weight in ounces of water daily, and consider adding electrolytes to your water to help support optimal hydration and mineral balance.

Another aspect of physical preparation is gradually adjusting your current diet in the weeks leading up to your official start date. Begin by reducing your intake of processed foods, added sugars, and refined carbohydrates, and focus on increasing your consumption of high-quality animal proteins and healthy fats. This gradual transition can help to minimize the potential for digestive discomfort and can make the overall transition to the carnivore diet feel less abrupt and overwhelming.

It is also wise to consult with a qualified healthcare professional before beginning the carnivore diet, particularly if you have any pre-existing health conditions or concerns. Your doctor can provide personalized guidance and can help you to monitor your health and make any necessary adjustments to your plan as you progress.

Carnivore Diet Food List: What to Eat and What to Avoid

When embarking on the carnivore diet, it's crucial to have a clear understanding of what foods to include and which ones to avoid. By focusing on nutrient-dense animal products and eliminating plant-based foods, you can optimize your health and experience the full benefits of this way of eating. Let's dive into the carnivore diet food list, exploring the various options available and the foods you should steer clear of.

The foundation of the carnivore diet revolves around high-quality animal products. Red meat, such as beef, lamb, and pork, should form the backbone of your meals. When possible, opt for grass-fed and pasture-raised meats, as they tend to have a more favorable nutrient profile, with higher levels of omega-3 fatty acids and vitamins. Don't be afraid to consume fatty cuts of meat, as they provide essential nutrients and help keep you satiated.

Poultry, including chicken, turkey, and duck, can also be enjoyed on the carnivore diet. Like red meat, aim for pasture-raised and organic options whenever possible. Feel free to consume both white and dark meat, as well as the skin, which is rich in healthy fats and flavor.

Organ meats, often referred to as "nature's multivitamins," are a must-include in your carnivore diet food list. Liver, heart, kidney, and other organ meats are packed with essential nutrients, such as vitamin A, B vitamins, iron, and CoQ10. Incorporating these nutrient-dense foods into your meals can help ensure you're meeting your body's nutritional needs.

Fish and seafood are excellent additions to the carnivore diet. Fatty fish, such as salmon, sardines, and mackerel, are particularly beneficial due to their high content of omega-3 fatty acids, which support brain health, reduce inflammation, and promote overall well-being. Shellfish, like oysters, clams, and mussels, are also nutrient powerhouses, providing zinc, selenium, and other essential minerals.

Eggs are a versatile and nutritious option on the carnivore diet. Rich in high-quality protein, healthy fats, and various vitamins and minerals, eggs can be enjoyed in numerous ways, from scrambled and poached to hard-boiled and fried. Don't discard the yolks, as they contain the majority of the egg's nutrients.

Dairy products, such as butter, ghee, and heavy cream, can be included in moderation on the carnivore diet. These foods provide a source of healthy fats and can add flavor and richness to your meals. However, some individuals may have sensitivities to dairy, so it's essential to listen to your body and adjust your intake accordingly.

While the focus is on animal products, there are some plant-based foods that you should avoid on the carnivore diet. Grains, including wheat, rice, and oats, are off-limits, as they can contribute to inflammation and digestive issues. Legumes, such as beans, lentils, and peanuts, should also be eliminated, as they contain antinutrients that can interfere with nutrient absorption.

Vegetables and fruits are typically excluded from the carnivore diet, as they contain plant toxins and antinutrients that can trigger inflammation and digestive distress in some individuals. While these foods may offer some nutritional benefits, the carnivore diet focuses on obtaining nutrients from animal sources, which are generally more bioavailable and easily absorbed by the body.

Processed foods, such as chips, crackers, and baked goods, have no place in the carnivore diet. These foods are often high in refined carbohydrates, unhealthy fats, and artificial ingredients that can derail your progress and undermine your health goals. Stick to whole, unprocessed animal foods to reap the full benefits of the carnivore lifestyle.

Sourcing High-Quality Animal Products

In the pursuit of optimal health through the Carnivore Diet, the quality of the animal products you consume is of utmost importance. Sourcing high-quality meat, eggs, and dairy is not just a matter of taste preference; it directly impacts the nutrient density of your meals and, consequently, your overall well-being. The old adage "you are what you eat" takes on a profound meaning when you consider that the animals you consume have their own unique diets and living conditions, which ultimately affect the quality of the food on your plate.

When embarking on the Carnivore Diet, it's essential to prioritize the sourcing of grass-fed and pasture-raised animal products whenever possible. These animals are raised in their natural environments, grazing on lush green pastures and basking in the sunlight, as nature intended. The resulting meat, eggs, and dairy are not only more flavorful but also pack a nutritional punch that far surpasses their conventionally raised counterparts.

Grass-fed beef, for example, boasts a more favorable fatty acid profile, with higher levels of anti-inflammatory omega-3 fatty acids and conjugated linoleic acid (CLA), a potent antioxidant. These beneficial fats contribute to heart health, brain function, and overall inflammation reduction. In contrast, conventionally raised cattle, often confined to feedlots and fed a diet of grains and soy, produce meat with a less desirable fatty acid composition and a lower nutrient density.

Pasture-raised eggs are another nutritional powerhouse that should be a staple in your Carnivore Diet. Hens raised on pasture have access to a diverse array of nutrients from foraging on insects, seeds, and green vegetation. As a result, their eggs contain higher levels of vitamins A, D, and E, as well as omega-3 fatty acids, compared to eggs from caged hens fed a grain-based diet. The vibrant orange yolks of pasture-raised eggs are a testament to their superior nutrient content and flavor.

When it comes to sourcing high-quality animal products, it's crucial to look beyond the labels and buzzwords. Terms like "natural," "free-range," and "organic" can be misleading, as they don't always guarantee the animals were raised in optimal conditions. Instead, seek out local farmers and ranchers who are transparent about their farming practices and prioritize the well-being of their animals. Building relationships with these producers not only ensures you have access to the highest quality animal products but also supports sustainable and ethical farming practices.

If you have the means and space, consider sourcing your animal products directly from local farmers through cow-sharing or community-supported agriculture (CSA) programs. These arrangements allow you to invest in a share of an animal or a portion of a farm's production, giving you access to the freshest and most nutrient-dense meat, eggs, and dairy available. You'll have the satisfaction of knowing exactly where your food comes from and how it was raised.

For those who don't have access to local farms or CSA programs, there are still options for sourcing high-quality animal products. Online retailers specializing in grass-fed and pasture-raised meats have become increasingly popular, offering a convenient way to have these premium products delivered right to your doorstep. When shopping online, look for reputable companies that prioritize transparency and sustainability, and read customer reviews to ensure the quality of the products meets your expectations.

In addition to sourcing grass-fed and pasture-raised animal products, it's important to consider the variety of cuts and organs you incorporate into your Carnivore Diet. While muscle meats like steak and ground beef are the foundation of the diet, organ meats, such as liver, heart, and kidney, offer a concentrated dose of essential nutrients that are often lacking in modern diets. Incorporating these nutrient-dense "superfoods" can help ensure you're getting a wide spectrum of vitamins, minerals, and beneficial compounds to support optimal health.

When sourcing organ meats, it's especially important to choose grass-fed and pasture-raised options, as the living conditions and diet of the animals have a significant impact on the quality and safety of these products. Organ meats from conventionally raised animals may contain higher levels of toxins and contaminants due to their exposure to pesticides, antibiotics, and other chemicals used in industrial farming practices.

Another aspect to consider when sourcing animal products is the use of antibiotics and hormones. Conventionally raised animals are often given routine antibiotics to prevent disease and promote growth, which can contribute to the development of antibiotic-resistant bacteria. Similarly, growth hormones are sometimes used to increase meat production, but they can have unintended consequences for both animal and human health. When possible, choose animal products from farmers who prioritize natural and holistic approaches to animal health and avoid the use of unnecessary antibiotics and hormones.

Lastly, don't underestimate the power of your local butcher or meat market when it comes to sourcing high-quality animal products. These professionals often have established relationships with local farmers and can provide valuable insights into the sourcing and quality of their products. They can also help you discover new cuts of meat and offer advice on preparation techniques to make the most of your Carnivore Diet meals.

In the end, sourcing high-quality animal products is an investment in your health and well-being. By prioritizing grass-fed and pasture-raised options, seeking out transparent and sustainable farming practices, and incorporating a variety of nutrient-dense cuts and organs, you'll be setting yourself up for success on your Carnivore Diet journey. The extra effort and cost associated with sourcing premium animal products are more than worth it when you consider the profound impact they can have on your energy levels, digestion, and overall vitality. So, take the time to research, build relationships, and make informed choices when it comes to the animal products you consume, and watch as your health transforms from the inside out.

Carnivore Diet Meal Planning and Preparation

Embarking on the carnivore diet requires a shift in mindset and a new approach to meal planning and preparation. While the diet may seem straightforward, consisting solely of animal products, it is essential to ensure that you are consuming a variety of high-quality, nutrient-dense foods to support your health and well-being. In this chapter, we will explore practical strategies and tips for effective meal planning and preparation on the carnivore diet.

First and foremost, it is crucial to prioritize the sourcing of high-quality animal products. Seek out grass-fed and grass-finished beef, pasture-raised poultry and pork, and wild-caught fish whenever possible. These animals, raised in their natural environments and on their species-appropriate diets, tend to have a more favorable nutrient profile, with higher levels of omega-3 fatty acids, vitamins, and minerals. Building relationships with local farmers, butchers, and fishmongers can help you access the best quality meats and ensure a consistent supply for your meal planning needs.

When it comes to meal preparation, simplicity is key. Focus on cooking methods that highlight the natural flavors of the animal products, such as grilling, roasting, sautéing, and slow-cooking. Experiment with different cuts of meat, including organ meats like liver and heart, to diversify your nutrient intake and keep your meals interesting. Incorporate bone broth, a rich source of collagen, minerals, and amino acids, into your meal plans by simmering bones, joints, and connective tissues for several hours.

Batch cooking can be a lifesaver when following the carnivore diet. Dedicate some time each week to preparing larger quantities of meat, which can be portioned out and reheated for quick and easy meals throughout the week. For example, slow-cook a large roast or braise tough cuts of meat like chuck or brisket, which can be shredded and used in various dishes. Grill or roast several chicken breasts or thighs at once, providing a convenient protein source for salads, wraps, or standalone meals.

Meal planning on the carnivore diet also involves ensuring that you have a variety of convenient, ready-to-eat options on hand. Keep hardboiled eggs, canned fish like salmon or sardines, and jerky or meat sticks in your fridge or pantry for snacks or quick meals on the go. Invest in quality storage containers and a vacuum sealer to preserve the freshness and quality of your pre-cooked meats and make meal prep more efficient.

To add variety and interest to your carnivore meals, experiment with different seasoning and marinade options that comply with the diet's guidelines. Salt, pepper, garlic, and herbs like rosemary and thyme can enhance the natural flavors of meat without adding any non-carnivore ingredients. Sugar-free and additive-free hot sauces, mustards, and mayos can also provide a flavorful kick to your dishes.

Consider incorporating intermittent fasting into your carnivore diet meal planning. By limiting your eating window to a specific timeframe each day, you can optimize digestion, promote fat burning, and simplify your meal prep routine. Many carnivore dieters find success with a 16/8 fasting protocol, where they eat during an 8-hour window and fast for the remaining 16 hours.

When dining out or attending social gatherings, plan ahead to ensure that you have carnivore-friendly options available. Research restaurant menus in advance and identify dishes that can be easily modified to fit your dietary needs, such as steak or grilled fish with no added sauces or seasonings. When attending events or gatherings, offer to bring a carnivore-compliant dish to share, ensuring that you have at least one option that aligns with your way of eating.

Transitioning to the Carnivore Diet: Tips and Strategies

Transitioning to the carnivore diet can be a significant change for many people, as it involves eliminating all plant-based foods and focusing solely on animal products. While the prospect of adopting this unconventional way of eating may seem daunting, there are several tips and strategies that can help make the transition smoother and more manageable. By preparing mentally and physically, and having a clear plan in place, you can set yourself up for success on your carnivore diet journey.

One of the first steps in transitioning to the carnivore diet is to educate yourself about the principles and guidelines of the approach. Take the time to read books, articles, and testimonials from experienced carnivore diet followers to gain a deeper understanding of what the diet entails and what to expect during the transition period. This knowledge will help you make informed decisions about your food choices and provide a foundation for navigating any challenges that may arise along the way.

Another important aspect of successfully transitioning to the carnivore diet is to start gradually. While some people may choose to dive in headfirst and eliminate all plant foods at once, this approach can be overwhelming and may lead to unpleasant side effects, such as digestive discomfort or cravings. Instead, consider a more gradual approach, slowly reducing your intake of plant-based foods over the course of a few weeks while increasing your consumption of high-quality animal products. This can help your body adapt to the new way of eating and minimize potential discomfort.

When transitioning to the carnivore diet, it is essential to focus on consuming a variety of nutrient-dense animal foods. While some carnivore diet followers may choose to focus primarily on beef, incorporating a range of animal products can help ensure that you are getting a well-rounded intake of essential nutrients. Consider including foods such as organ meats, eggs, fish, and dairy products (if tolerated) to provide a diverse array of vitamins, minerals, and beneficial compounds. Experimenting with different cuts of meat and cooking methods can also help keep your meals interesting and enjoyable.

Proper preparation is key to making the transition to the carnivore diet as smooth as possible. Take the time to plan your meals in advance, ensuring that you have a variety of high-quality animal products on hand. This can help reduce the temptation to reach for non-carnivore foods when hunger strikes. It is also a good idea to have some quick and easy meal options available, such as hard-boiled eggs or pre-cooked meat, for times when you are short on time or energy.

During the transition period, it is normal to experience some temporary side effects, often referred to as the "carnivore flu." These may include fatigue, headaches, irritability, and digestive issues. While these symptoms can be uncomfortable, they are typically short-lived and are a sign that your body is adapting to the new way of eating. To help manage these side effects, be sure to stay well-hydrated, get plenty of rest, and listen to your body's needs. If symptoms persist or become severe, consult with a healthcare professional to rule out any underlying health issues.

One of the most important factors in successfully transitioning to the carnivore diet is having a strong support system in place. Surround yourself with like-minded individuals who understand and support your dietary choices. Join online communities or social media groups dedicated to the carnivore diet, where you can connect with others who are on a similar journey, share experiences, and seek advice when needed. Having a network of support can provide motivation, accountability, and encouragement throughout your transition and beyond.

Overcoming Common Challenges and Obstacles

Adopting a carnivore diet can be a transformative experience, but it is not without its challenges and obstacles. Many individuals who embark on this unconventional dietary journey find themselves faced with a variety of hurdles, from social pressures to cravings for non-carnivore foods. However, with the right strategies and mindset, it is possible to overcome these challenges and maintain a successful and sustainable carnivore lifestyle.

One of the most common challenges faced by those new to the carnivore diet is navigating social situations that involve food. From family gatherings to dining out with friends, it can be difficult to stick to a strict animal-based diet when surrounded by tempting plant-based options. To overcome this challenge, it is essential to plan ahead and communicate your dietary needs clearly and confidently. When attending social events, offer to bring a carnivore-friendly dish to share, or research restaurant menus in advance to identify suitable options. Remember that your health and well-being are your top priorities, and don't be afraid to advocate for yourself and your dietary choices.

Another obstacle that many carnivore dieters face is the temptation to indulge in non-carnivore foods, particularly during times of stress or emotional upheaval. To combat these cravings, it is important to have a variety of satisfying and nutrient-dense carnivore options on hand at all times. Keep your kitchen stocked with high-quality meats, eggs, and other animal products, and experiment with different cooking methods and seasonings to keep your meals interesting and enjoyable. When cravings strike, take a moment to check in with yourself and identify the underlying emotional or physical need that may be driving the desire for non-carnivore foods. Often, a glass of water, a quick walk, or a few deep breaths can help to alleviate cravings and keep you on track.

For some individuals, the transition to a carnivore diet can also be accompanied by digestive discomfort or other physical symptoms, such as fatigue or headaches. These symptoms are often referred to as the "adaptation phase" and are a normal part of the body's adjustment to a new way of eating. To minimize discomfort and support your body through this transition, it is essential to prioritize hydration, electrolyte balance, and high-quality sleep. Consider incorporating bone broth or other nutrient-dense liquids into your diet to support gut health and reduce inflammation. If symptoms persist or become severe, don't hesitate to reach out to a qualified healthcare professional for guidance and support.

Another common challenge faced by carnivore dieters is the perception that the diet is expensive or difficult to maintain on a budget. While it is true that high-quality animal products can be more costly than processed or plant-based foods, there are many strategies for making the carnivore diet more affordable. One approach is to purchase meat in bulk from local farmers or online suppliers, taking advantage of sales and discounts when possible. Another strategy is to prioritize less expensive cuts of meat, such as ground beef or organ meats, which are often more nutrient-dense than pricier cuts. With a little creativity and planning, it is possible to maintain a carnivore diet without breaking the bank.

CHAPTER 3

THRIVING ON THE CARNIVORE DIET

Listening to Your Body and Adjusting Your Approach

Embarking on the carnivore diet is a profound journey of self-discovery, one that requires a keen awareness of your body's unique needs and responses. As you navigate this new way of eating, it's crucial to develop a deep sense of self-awareness and learn to listen to the subtle messages your body sends you. By tuning in to these signals and making adjustments accordingly, you can optimize your carnivore diet experience and unlock the full potential of this transformative lifestyle.

One of the first things to pay attention to when starting the carnivore diet is how your body reacts to different types of animal products. While some individuals may thrive on a diet rich in red meat, others may find that they feel better incorporating more poultry, fish, or eggs into their meals. Take note of how you feel after consuming different animal foods, both in terms of energy levels and digestive comfort. If you notice that certain foods consistently leave you feeling sluggish or cause digestive distress, it may be a sign to adjust your protein sources and experiment with other options.

Another important aspect of listening to your body on the carnivore diet is monitoring your hunger and satiety signals. Unlike many other diets that rely on strict portion control or calorie counting, the carnivore diet encourages you to eat intuitively, consuming animal foods until you feel satisfied. Pay attention to the natural ebbs and flows of your appetite, and allow yourself to eat when you're truly hungry, rather than adhering to a rigid meal schedule. At the same time, be mindful of overeating, as consuming excessive amounts of protein and fat can lead to digestive discomfort and stall your progress.

As you become more attuned to your body's needs, you may also notice that your preferences for certain cuts of meat or cooking methods evolve over time. Some individuals may find that they crave fattier cuts of meat, such as ribeye or bacon, while others may prefer leaner options, like sirloin or chicken breast. Similarly, you may discover that you enjoy your meats cooked to a specific doneness or that certain preparation methods, such as grilling or slow-cooking, enhance your enjoyment and satisfaction. Don't be afraid to experiment with different cuts, cooking techniques, and seasoning options to find what works best for you.

In addition to the physical aspects of the carnivore diet, it's essential to be attuned to the emotional and mental impacts of this way of eating. For some, the simplicity and strictness of the carnivore diet can be liberating, eliminating the stress and decision fatigue that often accompany more complex dietary approaches. However, others may find the limitations of the diet mentally challenging, particularly in social situations or when dining out. If you find yourself struggling with the emotional aspects of the carnivore diet, it's important to acknowledge these feelings and seek support from others who understand your journey.

One way to ensure that you're listening to your body and making necessary adjustments is to keep a food and symptom journal. Record the animal foods you consume each day, along with any physical, mental, or emotional symptoms you experience. Over time, patterns may emerge that can help you identify which foods make you feel your best and which ones may be contributing to any challenges you face. This information can be invaluable in fine-tuning your carnivore diet approach and ensuring that you're meeting your individual needs.

It's also crucial to remember that the carnivore diet is not a one-size-fits-all approach. What works for one person may not work for another, and it's essential to be patient and compassionate with yourself as you navigate this new way of eating. If you find that certain aspects of the carnivore diet are not serving you, don't be afraid to make adjustments or seek guidance from a knowledgeable healthcare professional. The ultimate goal is to find a sustainable and nourishing approach that supports your unique body and enables you to thrive.

Optimizing Nutrient Intake on the Carnivore Diet

Embarking on the Carnivore Diet is a journey of self-discovery, as you learn to nourish your body with the most nutrient-dense foods nature has to offer. While the concept of eating only animal products may seem straightforward, there is an art and science to optimizing your nutrient intake to ensure you're getting everything your body needs to thrive. By focusing on high-quality animal products, incorporating a variety of cuts and organs, and being mindful of your individual needs, you can unlock the full potential of the Carnivore Diet and experience a profound transformation in your health and well-being.

At the core of optimizing nutrient intake on the Carnivore Diet is the principle of nose-to-tail eating. This means going beyond the familiar muscle meats and embracing the whole animal, including organs, bones, and connective tissues. Each part of the animal offers a unique array of nutrients, and by incorporating a diverse range of cuts into your meals, you'll be providing your body with a comprehensive spectrum of vitamins, minerals, and beneficial compounds.

Organ meats, in particular, are the unsung heroes of the Carnivore Diet. These nutrient-dense "superfoods" are packed with essential vitamins, minerals, and other compounds that are often lacking in modern diets. Liver, for example, is one of the most nutrient-dense foods on the planet, offering high levels of vitamin A, B vitamins, iron, copper, and zinc. Heart is an excellent source of CoQ10, a powerful antioxidant that supports cardiovascular health, while kidney provides a rich source of selenium, a mineral essential for thyroid function and immune health.

Incorporating organ meats into your Carnivore Diet may take some getting used to, especially if you're not accustomed to their unique flavors and textures. Start by incorporating small amounts of liver or heart into your ground beef dishes, or try a classic liver and onions recipe. As you become more comfortable with these nutrient-dense foods, you can experiment with different preparation methods and incorporate a wider variety of organs into your meals.

In addition to organ meats, it's important to include a variety of muscle cuts in your Carnivore Diet. Each cut of meat offers a unique nutrient profile, and by rotating your protein sources, you'll ensure you're getting a well-rounded intake of essential amino acids, fats, and micronutrients. For example, ribeye steak is renowned for its high fat content and rich flavor, while sirloin is a leaner cut that offers a good balance of protein and fat. Slow-cooked roasts and stews are a great way to incorporate tougher cuts like chuck or brisket, which are rich in collagen and other beneficial compounds that support gut health and joint function.

When it comes to optimizing nutrient intake, the quality of your animal products is just as important as the variety. Prioritizing grass-fed and pasture-raised meats, eggs, and dairy ensures that you're getting the most nutrient-dense options available. These animals are raised in their natural environments, foraging on a diverse array of plants and insects, which results in a more favorable nutrient profile compared to conventionally raised animals. Grass-fed beef, for example, has higher levels of omega-3 fatty acids, CLA, and vitamin E, while pasture-raised eggs boast richer yolks and higher levels of vitamins A and D.

Another aspect of optimizing nutrient intake on the Carnivore Diet is being mindful of your individual needs and goals. While the core principles of the diet remain the same, there is room for personalization based on factors such as age, gender, activity level, and health status. For example, athletes or individuals with higher energy demands may need to consume more fat to support their increased caloric needs, while those with specific health concerns may benefit from emphasizing certain nutrient-dense foods or limiting others.

It's also important to listen to your body and pay attention to how you feel as you navigate the Carnivore Diet. Some people may thrive on a higher fat intake, while others may feel better with a more moderate approach. If you find yourself experiencing digestive discomfort or other symptoms, it may be worth experimenting with different cuts of meat, cooking methods, or even eliminating certain foods temporarily to identify any potential intolerances.

Optimizing nutrient intake on the Carnivore Diet is an ongoing process of experimentation, adaptation, and refinement. As you become more attuned to your body's needs and preferences, you'll develop a deeper understanding of how to nourish yourself optimally. Keep a food journal to track your meals, symptoms, and energy levels, and don't be afraid to make adjustments as needed.

In addition to the foods you eat, there are other factors that can influence your nutrient intake on the Carnivore Diet. Proper food handling and preparation techniques are essential for preserving the nutrient content of your animal products. Overcooking meats, for example, can lead to the formation of harmful compounds and the loss of heat-sensitive vitamins. Opt for gentler cooking methods like slow roasting, braising, or pan-searing to maintain the integrity of your food.

Supplementation can also play a role in optimizing nutrient intake on the Carnivore Diet, particularly for those with specific health concerns or dietary restrictions. While the goal should always be to obtain nutrients from whole foods whenever possible, targeted supplementation can help fill any potential gaps. Common supplements on the Carnivore Diet include electrolytes like sodium, potassium, and magnesium, as well as vitamin D, which can be difficult to obtain from food sources alone. However, it's crucial to consult with a qualified healthcare professional before starting any new supplement regimen to ensure safety and appropriateness for your individual needs.

Ultimately, optimizing nutrient intake on the Carnivore Diet is a personal journey that requires patience, curiosity, and a willingness to adapt. By prioritizing high-quality animal products, incorporating a diverse range of cuts and organs, and being attuned to your body's unique needs, you'll be well on your way to experiencing the transformative power of this way of eating. Embrace the process of self-discovery, trust in the wisdom of your body, and watch as your health and vitality soar to new heights.

Incorporating Organ Meats and Bone Broth

Organ meats and bone broth are two of the most nutrient-dense and beneficial components of the carnivore diet. These often-overlooked foods are true superfoods, packed with essential vitamins, minerals, and compounds that support overall health and well-being. Incorporating organ meats and bone broth into your carnivore meal plan can help ensure that you are obtaining a wide range of nutrients and maximizing the potential benefits of this way of eating.

Organ meats, such as liver, heart, kidney, and tongue, are some of the most nutrient-dense foods on the planet. These meats are rich in vitamins A, B12, D, E, and K2, as well as minerals like iron, zinc, and copper. Liver, in particular, is an excellent source of preformed vitamin A, which is essential for immune function, eye health, and skin health. It also contains high levels of folate, choline, and coenzyme Q10, which support brain function and energy production.

Incorporating organ meats into your carnivore diet can be as simple as adding a small portion of liver or heart to your weekly meal plan. Start with a small amount, such as 1-2 ounces per serving, and gradually increase as your taste buds adapt. If you find the flavor of organ meats too strong, try soaking them in milk or lemon juice for a few hours before cooking to help mellow out the taste. You can also mix ground organ meats with regular ground beef or pork to create flavorful and nutrient-dense patties, meatballs, or sausages.

Bone broth, made by simmering bones, joints, and connective tissues for several hours, is another essential component of the carnivore diet. This nutrient-rich liquid is an excellent source of collagen, gelatin, and amino acids like proline and glycine, which support gut health, joint function, and skin elasticity. Bone broth also contains minerals like calcium, magnesium, and phosphorus, which are essential for bone health and overall physiological function.

To make bone broth, simply save bones and connective tissues from your carnivore meals, such as chicken carcasses, beef marrow bones, or pork knuckles. Place the bones in a large pot or slow cooker, cover with water, and add a splash of apple cider vinegar to help extract the nutrients from the bones. Simmer the broth on low heat for 12-48 hours, depending on the type of bones used and the desired flavor and consistency. Strain the broth and store it in glass jars or freezer-safe containers for later use.

Bone broth can be consumed on its own as a warm and comforting beverage, or used as a base for soups, stews, and sauces. It can also be used to braise meats or cook vegetables, adding depth of flavor and additional nutrients to your meals. Aim to consume at least 1-2 cups of bone broth per day to reap the maximum benefits for your health.

When sourcing organ meats and bones for broth, it is essential to choose high-quality, grass-fed, and pasture-raised animals whenever possible. These animals, raised in their natural environments and on their species-appropriate diets, tend to have a more favorable nutrient profile and fewer toxins compared to conventionally-raised animals. Building relationships with local farmers, butchers, and specialty meat suppliers can help you access the best quality organ meats and bones for your carnivore diet.

If you are new to consuming organ meats and bone broth, start slowly and listen to your body's feedback. Some people may experience digestive discomfort or other symptoms when first introducing these foods, particularly if they have a history of gut issues or food sensitivities. If you experience any adverse reactions, reduce your intake or consult with a qualified healthcare professional to determine the best approach for your individual needs.

In addition to their nutrient density and potential health benefits, organ meats and bone broth can add variety and interest to your carnivore meal plan. Experiment with different recipes and preparation methods, such as liver pâté, grilled heart skewers, or slow-cooker bone broth, to keep your meals exciting and satisfying.

The Role of Salt and Electrolytes on the Carnivore Diet

The carnivore diet, which consists solely of animal products, has gained popularity in recent years for its potential health benefits. However, one crucial aspect of this way of eating that is often overlooked is the role of salt and electrolytes. When eliminating plant foods from the diet, it is essential to pay close attention to these nutrients to ensure optimal health and well-being. Understanding the importance of salt and electrolytes on the carnivore diet can help you make informed decisions about your food choices and maintain proper balance in your body.

Salt, or sodium chloride, is a vital nutrient that plays a key role in many bodily functions. It helps regulate fluid balance, supports nerve and muscle function, and aids in the absorption of other nutrients. On a conventional diet that includes plant foods, sodium is often abundant due to the presence of processed foods and added salt. However, on the carnivore diet, which emphasizes whole, unprocessed animal products, sodium intake may be lower than what the body requires. This is because most animal products, with the exception of some seafood, are relatively low in sodium.

To ensure adequate sodium intake on the carnivore diet, it is important to be intentional about adding salt to your meals. This can be done by seasoning your meat and other animal products with high-quality sea salt or Himalayan pink salt, which also contain trace minerals that can support overall health. Some carnivore diet followers also choose to drink bone broth or consume salted butter to increase their sodium intake. It is important to listen to your body's cues and adjust your salt intake based on factors such as your activity level, sweat rate, and any underlying health conditions.

In addition to sodium, other electrolytes, such as potassium, magnesium, and calcium, also play crucial roles in maintaining proper bodily functions. These minerals help regulate fluid balance, support heart health, and are essential for bone density and muscle function. While animal products do contain some of these electrolytes, the amounts may be lower than what is found in plant-based foods. This is particularly true for potassium, which is abundant in fruits and vegetables but less so in animal products.

To ensure adequate intake of these essential electrolytes on the carnivore diet, it is important to include a variety of animal foods in your meals. Organ meats, such as liver and kidney, are particularly rich in nutrients, including electrolytes. Dairy products, if tolerated, can also be a good source of calcium and magnesium. Some carnivore diet followers choose to supplement with electrolyte powders or drops to help meet their needs, particularly if they are engaging in high-intensity exercise or sweating heavily.

It is worth noting that the body's electrolyte needs can vary depending on individual factors, such as age, gender, activity level, and health status. Some people may be more prone to electrolyte imbalances, particularly if they have certain medical conditions or take medications that affect mineral balance. If you are considering the carnivore diet and have concerns about your electrolyte needs, it is important to consult with a healthcare professional who can provide personalized guidance and monitor your nutrient status.

One potential challenge of ensuring adequate electrolyte intake on the carnivore diet is the lack of variety in food choices. When eliminating plant foods, it can be easy to fall into a routine of eating the same animal products repeatedly. This can lead to taste fatigue and make it more challenging to meet your nutrient needs. To avoid this, try to incorporate a range of animal foods into your meals, experimenting with different cuts of meat, organ meats, and seafood. You can also vary your cooking methods and seasoning to keep your meals interesting and enjoyable.

Another important consideration when it comes to salt and electrolytes on the carnivore diet is the quality of the products you consume. When possible, choose high-quality, minimally processed animal foods, such as grass-fed beef, pasture-raised eggs, and wild-caught fish. These products may be more nutrient-dense and contain a more favorable balance of electrolytes compared to their conventionally raised counterparts. Additionally, be mindful of any added ingredients in processed meat products, such as cured meats or sausages, which may contain high amounts of sodium or other additives that can affect electrolyte balance.

Staying Hydrated on the Carnivore Diet

Maintaining proper hydration is a crucial aspect of any healthy lifestyle, and it becomes even more important when following a carnivore diet. As you eliminate plant-based foods, which can be a significant source of dietary water, it is essential to pay close attention to your fluid intake to ensure that your body is functioning optimally. In this chapter, we will explore the importance of hydration on the carnivore diet and provide practical tips for staying properly hydrated.

When you adopt a carnivore diet, your body undergoes a significant metabolic shift as it adapts to using fat and protein as its primary fuel sources. During this adaptation phase, which can last anywhere from a few weeks to a few months, your body may excrete more water than usual as it burns through its stored glycogen and adjusts to a lower carbohydrate intake. This increased water loss can lead to dehydration if not properly addressed, resulting in symptoms such as fatigue, headaches, and constipation.

To combat dehydration and support your body's needs on the carnivore diet, it is essential to make a conscious effort to drink enough fluids throughout the day. A good rule of thumb is to aim for at least half your body weight in ounces of water per day. For example, if you weigh 150 pounds, you should strive to drink at least 75 ounces of water daily. However, this is just a general guideline, and your individual hydration needs may vary depending on factors such as your activity level, climate, and overall health status.

In addition to plain water, there are several other carnivore-friendly options for staying hydrated. Bone broth, which is made by simmering animal bones and connective tissues in water for an extended period, is an excellent source of both hydration and nutrition. Bone broth is rich in minerals such as calcium, magnesium, and phosphorus, as well as amino acids like glycine and proline, which can support gut health and reduce inflammation. Sipping on bone broth throughout the day can help to keep you hydrated while also providing a comforting and nourishing beverage option.

Another important aspect of hydration on the carnivore diet is ensuring that you are consuming enough electrolytes. Electrolytes are essential minerals such as sodium, potassium, and magnesium that help to regulate fluid balance, nerve function, and muscle contractions in the body. When you eliminate plant-based foods, which can be a significant source of dietary electrolytes, it becomes even more crucial to ensure that you are getting enough of these minerals through your carnivore food choices.

One way to increase your electrolyte intake on the carnivore diet is to season your meals generously with high-quality sea salt. Unlike refined table salt, sea salt contains trace minerals that can help to support proper hydration and electrolyte balance. Don't be afraid to use salt liberally on your meats and other carnivore foods, as your body's need for sodium may increase on this low-carbohydrate way of eating.

You can also support your electrolyte needs by incorporating nutrient-dense animal foods into your carnivore diet. Fatty fish like salmon and sardines are rich in potassium and magnesium, while organ meats such as liver and kidney are excellent sources of a wide range of essential minerals. Eating a variety of high-quality animal products can help to ensure that you are getting the full spectrum of nutrients needed to support optimal hydration and overall health.

In addition to consuming enough fluids and electrolytes, there are several other strategies you can use to support hydration on the carnivore diet. One simple tip is to carry a reusable water bottle with you throughout the day, and make a habit of sipping on it regularly. You can also set reminders on your phone or computer to prompt you to drink water at regular intervals, or use a hydration tracking app to monitor your fluid intake and ensure that you are meeting your daily goals.

Another helpful strategy is to pay attention to your body's thirst signals and drink water when you feel thirsty, rather than waiting until you are already dehydrated. Thirst is your body's way of telling you that it needs more fluids, so it is important to listen to these cues and respond accordingly. If you find that you are often too busy or distracted to notice your thirst signals, try setting aside specific times throughout the day to focus on hydration, such as first thing in the morning, before meals, and before and after exercise.

It is also important to be mindful of situations that may increase your hydration needs, such as hot weather, high altitudes, and intense physical activity. In these cases, you may need to increase your fluid intake even further to compensate for increased water loss through sweat and respiration. If you are engaging in prolonged or strenuous exercise, consider adding an electrolyte supplement to your water to help replenish lost minerals and support optimal hydration.

Amanda Quinn

CHAPTER 4

THE CARNIVORE DIET FOR SPECIFIC GOALS AND CONDITIONS

The Carnivore Diet for Weight Loss

The carnivore diet has gained significant attention in recent years as a powerful tool for weight loss. By focusing on nutrient-dense animal products and eliminating plant-based foods, many individuals have experienced remarkable results in shedding excess body fat and improving their overall body composition. Let's explore the mechanisms behind the carnivore diet's effectiveness for weight loss and how you can harness its potential to achieve your own goals.

One of the primary reasons the carnivore diet is so effective for weight loss is its ability to naturally regulate appetite and promote satiety. Animal products, particularly those high in protein and fat, are incredibly satiating, meaning they help you feel full and satisfied for longer periods. When you consume a meal rich in high-quality meat, eggs, or fish, your body releases hormones like ghrelin and peptide YY, which signal to your brain that you've had enough to eat. This natural appetite regulation can lead to a spontaneous reduction in calorie intake, making it easier to create the calorie deficit necessary for weight loss.

Moreover, the carnivore diet's emphasis on high-quality protein sources supports the preservation and growth of lean muscle mass. When you restrict your calorie intake to lose weight, your body may break down both fat and muscle tissue for energy. However, by consuming adequate amounts of protein, you provide your body with the building blocks it needs to maintain and even build muscle. This is crucial for weight loss, as muscle tissue is metabolically active, meaning it burns calories even at rest. By preserving your muscle mass, you can help keep your metabolism humming along, making it easier to shed unwanted body fat.

The elimination of carbohydrates on the carnivore diet also contributes to its weight loss potential. When you drastically reduce your carb intake, your body enters a metabolic state called ketosis, in which it begins to burn fat for fuel instead of relying on glucose from carbohydrates. This shift in fuel source can lead to a rapid and substantial loss of body fat, particularly in the initial stages of the diet. Additionally, the absence of carbs helps to stabilize blood sugar levels, reducing insulin spikes and the subsequent storage of excess calories as fat.

Another factor that makes the carnivore diet effective for weight loss is its simplicity and elimination of processed foods. By focusing on whole, unprocessed animal products, you naturally avoid many of the calorie-dense, nutrient-poor foods that can derail weight loss efforts. Processed foods, such as chips, cookies, and sugary beverages, are often high in refined carbohydrates, unhealthy fats, and added sugars, all of which can contribute to weight gain and metabolic dysfunction. By removing these foods from your diet and replacing them with nourishing animal products, you create an environment conducive to weight loss and improved overall health.

To maximize your weight loss potential on the carnivore diet, it's essential to prioritize high-quality animal products and listen to your body's hunger and satiety signals. Opt for grass-fed and pasture-raised meats, as they tend to have a more favorable nutrient profile and a better balance of omega-3 to omega-6 fatty acids. Incorporate a variety of animal foods, including red meat, poultry, fish, eggs, and organ meats, to ensure you're obtaining a wide range of essential nutrients. Pay attention to your body's natural hunger cues, and eat until you feel satisfied, rather than adhering to a strict calorie count or portion size.

It's also important to be patient and consistent with your efforts. While some individuals may experience rapid weight loss in the beginning, others may see a more gradual progression. Remember that sustainable weight loss is a journey, and the carnivore diet is a long-term approach to improving your health and body composition. Celebrate your successes along the way, and don't get discouraged if you encounter plateaus or challenges. With persistence and a commitment to nourishing your body with high-quality animal foods, you can achieve your weight loss goals and experience the transformative power of the carnivore diet.

The Carnivore Diet for Muscle Gain and Strength

The Carnivore Diet has gained a reputation not only for its potential health benefits but also for its ability to support muscle gain and strength. For those seeking to build a powerful physique and enhance their athletic performance, this way of eating offers a compelling approach that challenges conventional wisdom about nutrition and fitness. By focusing on nutrient-dense animal products and eliminating potentially inflammatory plant foods, the Carnivore Diet provides a solid foundation for muscle growth, recovery, and overall physical optimization.

At the heart of muscle gain and strength is the concept of protein intake. Protein is the building block of muscle tissue, and consuming adequate amounts is essential for supporting hypertrophy and repair. The Carnivore Diet is naturally high in high-quality, bioavailable protein, making it an ideal choice for those looking to pack on lean mass. Animal proteins, such as beef, pork, poultry, and fish, contain all the essential amino acids needed for muscle protein synthesis, the process by which the body builds and repairs muscle tissue.

One of the key advantages of the Carnivore Diet for muscle gain is its simplicity. By eliminating the need to track macronutrients or worry about food combinations, this approach allows you to focus on consuming enough protein and overall calories to support your goals. The high satiety factor of animal products also makes it easier to control appetite and avoid overeating, which can be a common pitfall when trying to gain muscle.

In addition to protein, the Carnivore Diet provides a rich source of other nutrients crucial for muscle growth and recovery. Creatine, for example, is a compound found naturally in meat that has been shown to enhance strength, power, and muscle mass. Consuming a diet rich in animal products ensures a steady supply of this potent performance-enhancer, without the need for supplementation.

Zinc, another essential nutrient for muscle growth, is also abundant in animal foods. This mineral plays a key role in testosterone production, a hormone that is critical for building and maintaining muscle mass. Adequate zinc intake has been linked to improved strength, recovery, and overall athletic performance. Red meat, in particular, is an excellent source of zinc, making it a staple food for those following the Carnivore Diet for muscle gain.

The high-fat nature of the Carnivore Diet can also be beneficial for muscle growth and strength. Healthy fats, such as those found in grass-fed beef and wild-caught fish, provide a concentrated source of energy that can support intense training sessions and recovery. Fats also play a role in hormone production, including testosterone, which is essential for muscle building. Consuming a diet rich in healthy fats can help optimize hormone levels and create an anabolic environment conducive to muscle growth.

Another often-overlooked benefit of the Carnivore Diet for muscle gain is its potential to reduce inflammation. Chronic inflammation can hinder muscle growth and recovery, as well as contribute to joint pain and stiffness. By eliminating potentially inflammatory plant foods, such as grains, legumes, and processed oils, the Carnivore Diet may help reduce systemic inflammation and create a more favorable environment for muscle building.

To optimize muscle gain and strength on the Carnivore Diet, it's important to focus on consuming a variety of high-quality animal products. Prioritize grass-fed and pasture-raised meats, as they tend to have a more favorable nutrient profile compared to conventionally raised animals. Incorporate a mix of muscle meats, organ meats, and connective tissues to ensure a comprehensive intake of essential nutrients.

In terms of meal frequency and timing, the Carnivore Diet offers flexibility based on individual preferences and goals. Some may thrive on a higher meal frequency, consuming smaller portions of meat throughout the day to maintain a steady supply of amino acids for muscle protein synthesis. Others may prefer a more intermittent fasting approach, consuming larger, less frequent meals to promote fat loss and insulin sensitivity. Experiment with different meal patterns to find what works best for your body and lifestyle.

Resistance training is a crucial component of building muscle and strength, and the Carnivore Diet can be an excellent complement to a well-designed workout program. Focus on compound exercises that target multiple muscle groups, such as squats, deadlifts, bench presses, and rows. Progressively increasing the weight and volume over time will stimulate muscle growth and strength gains. Be sure to allow adequate rest and recovery between training sessions to optimize muscle repair and adaptation.

Hydration is another key factor in muscle growth and performance. The high protein intake on the Carnivore Diet can increase fluid needs, so it's essential to consume enough water and electrolytes to support hydration and cellular function. Aim for at least half your body weight in ounces of water per day, and consider adding sea salt or an electrolyte supplement to your water to replenish minerals lost through sweat.

While the Carnivore Diet can be a powerful tool for muscle gain and strength, it's important to approach it with realistic expectations and a commitment to consistency. Building muscle takes time, patience, and dedication. Focus on making progress over perfection, and celebrate the small victories along the way. Keep a training log to track your workouts, and adjust your diet and training as needed based on your individual response and progress.

It's also crucial to listen to your body and prioritize overall health and well-being. While the Carnivore Diet can be beneficial for many, it may not be suitable for everyone. If you experience persistent fatigue, digestive issues, or other concerning symptoms, it may be worth reevaluating your approach or consulting with a qualified healthcare professional.

The Carnivore Diet for Digestive Health

The carnivore diet, which consists solely of animal products, has gained significant attention for its potential to support and improve digestive health. Many individuals who have struggled with chronic digestive issues, such as irritable bowel syndrome (IBS), inflammatory bowel disease (IBD), and leaky gut syndrome, have found relief and healing by adopting this unconventional way of eating. The carnivore diet's focus on nutrient-dense, easily digestible foods, coupled with the elimination of potential irritants and allergens, can create a powerful healing environment for the gut.

One of the primary reasons the carnivore diet can be so beneficial for digestive health is its elimination of plant-based foods, which can be difficult for some people to digest. Many plants contain compounds like lectins, phytates, and oxalates, which can interfere with nutrient absorption and irritate the gut lining. For example, lectins, found in high concentrations in grains and legumes, can bind to the cells of the intestinal wall and contribute to increased intestinal permeability, or "leaky gut." By removing these potential irritants, the carnivore diet allows the gut lining to heal and restore its integrity, reducing inflammation and improving overall digestive function.

The carnivore diet's emphasis on high-quality animal protein and fat can also support digestive health by providing the necessary building blocks for a healthy gut lining. Collagen, found in connective tissues and bone broth, is particularly important for maintaining the structure and function of the intestinal wall. Glycine, an amino acid abundant in collagen-rich foods, has been shown to reduce inflammation and support the production of stomach acid, which is essential for proper digestion and nutrient absorption. By consuming a variety of nutrient-dense animal products, including organ meats and bone broth, followers of the carnivore diet can nourish and strengthen their digestive system.

Another key aspect of the carnivore diet that can benefit digestive health is its low-fiber content. While fiber is often touted as essential for regular bowel movements and gut health, some individuals may have difficulty tolerating high-fiber diets, particularly those with pre-existing digestive issues. Fibrous plant foods can ferment in the large intestine, leading to bloating, gas, and discomfort for some people. By minimizing or eliminating fiber, the carnivore diet can provide relief for those with sensitive digestive systems and allow the gut to rest and heal.

The carnivore diet's potential to improve digestive health is further supported by its positive impact on the gut microbiome. While the exact mechanisms are still being researched, some studies suggest that a diet high in animal products can promote the growth of beneficial gut bacteria, such as Bifidobacteria and Lactobacillus species. These bacteria play a crucial role in maintaining gut barrier function, regulating inflammation, and supporting immune health. By fostering a healthy gut microbiome, the carnivore diet may help alleviate digestive symptoms and promote overall well-being.

To maximize the digestive health benefits of the carnivore diet, it is essential to focus on high-quality, nutrient-dense animal products. Prioritize grass-fed and pasture-raised meats, organ meats, and bone broth, as these foods contain higher levels of beneficial nutrients and fewer toxins compared to conventionally-raised animal products. Pay attention to your body's signals and adjust your food choices and portion sizes accordingly. Some individuals may benefit from a more gradual transition to the carnivore diet, starting with the elimination of the most problematic plant foods and slowly increasing their intake of animal products over time.

It is also important to note that while the carnivore diet can be a powerful tool for improving digestive health, it may not be suitable for everyone. Some individuals may have underlying health conditions or genetic factors that require a more diverse diet or specific nutrient interventions. If you have a history of digestive issues or other health concerns, it is always best to consult with a qualified healthcare professional before making significant dietary changes.

The Carnivore Diet for Autoimmune Conditions

The carnivore diet has gained attention in recent years as a potential therapeutic approach for individuals with autoimmune conditions. Autoimmune disorders occur when the body's immune system mistakenly attacks its own tissues, leading to chronic inflammation and a wide range of symptoms. While conventional treatments often focus on managing symptoms through medication, some people have found relief by adopting the carnivore diet, which eliminates all plant-based foods and focuses solely on animal products. By removing potential dietary triggers and providing a nutrient-dense approach to eating, the carnivore diet may offer hope for those struggling with autoimmune conditions.

One of the primary reasons the carnivore diet may be beneficial for autoimmune disorders is its ability to reduce inflammation in the body. Many plant foods, particularly those high in lectins, phytates, and other antinutrients, can contribute to intestinal permeability, or "leaky gut," which is thought to be a key factor in the development and progression of autoimmune conditions. When the gut lining becomes compromised, partially digested food particles and bacteria can enter the bloodstream, triggering an immune response and leading to systemic inflammation. By eliminating these potentially problematic plant foods, the carnivore diet may help heal the gut, reduce inflammation, and alleviate autoimmune symptoms.

The nutrient density of the carnivore diet may also play a role in its potential benefits for autoimmune conditions. Animal products, particularly organ meats and fatty fish, are rich in essential nutrients that support immune function and overall health. These include vitamins A, D, and B12, as well as minerals like zinc, iron, and selenium. By providing the body with a concentrated source of these nutrients, the carnivore diet may help support the immune system and promote healing in individuals with autoimmune disorders.

Another potential mechanism by which the carnivore diet may benefit autoimmune conditions is through its impact on the gut microbiome. The gut is home to trillions of bacteria that play a crucial role in immune function and overall health. Dysbiosis, or an imbalance in the gut microbiome, has been linked to the development and progression of autoimmune disorders. By eliminating many of the foods that can disrupt gut health, such as processed foods, refined carbohydrates, and plant-based antinutrients, the carnivore diet may help restore a healthy balance of gut bacteria. This, in turn, can support immune function and reduce inflammation throughout the body.

It is important to note that while anecdotal evidence suggests the carnivore diet may be helpful for some individuals with autoimmune conditions, scientific research on this topic is limited. More studies are needed to fully understand the potential benefits and risks of the carnivore diet for autoimmune disorders. Additionally, the elimination of entire food groups, particularly fruits and vegetables, may lead to nutrient deficiencies and other potential health concerns. It is crucial for individuals with autoimmune conditions to work closely with a healthcare professional when considering the carnivore diet to ensure that it is safe and appropriate for their specific needs.

When implementing the carnivore diet for autoimmune conditions, it is important to focus on high-quality, nutrient-dense animal products. This includes grass-fed and pasture-raised meats, organ meats, eggs, and wild-caught fish. These products are often higher in beneficial nutrients and may be less likely to contain harmful additives or contaminants that can exacerbate autoimmune symptoms. It is also important to listen to your body and pay attention to any potential reactions or sensitivities to specific animal products, as some individuals may have unique tolerances or intolerances.

In addition to dietary changes, individuals with autoimmune conditions may also benefit from other lifestyle modifications that support overall health and well-being. These may include stress management techniques, such as meditation or deep breathing exercises, regular physical activity, and adequate sleep. By taking a holistic approach to health and addressing both dietary and lifestyle factors, individuals with autoimmune conditions may be able to better manage their symptoms and improve their quality of life.

It is worth noting that the carnivore diet may not be suitable for everyone with an autoimmune condition, and individual responses may vary. Some people may find that they feel better on a more moderate approach that includes some plant foods, while others may thrive on a strict carnivore diet. It is important to approach any dietary change with caution and to monitor your symptoms and overall health closely. If you do not experience improvements or if your symptoms worsen on the carnivore diet, it may be necessary to reevaluate your approach and consider other dietary or lifestyle modifications.

The Carnivore Diet for Mental Health and Cognitive Function

The carnivore diet, with its emphasis on high-quality animal products and elimination of plant-based foods, has garnered significant attention in recent years for its potential benefits for physical health and well-being. However, an often-overlooked aspect of this unconventional way of eating is its potential impact on mental health and cognitive function. In this chapter, we will explore the ways in which the carnivore diet may support brain health, mood, and overall cognitive performance.

One of the primary ways in which the carnivore diet may benefit mental health is through its ability to reduce inflammation in the body and brain. Chronic inflammation has been linked to a wide range of mental health disorders, including depression, anxiety, and even neurodegenerative conditions like Alzheimer's disease. By eliminating potentially inflammatory plant-based foods and focusing on nutrient-dense animal products, the carnivore diet may help to reduce overall inflammation and support optimal brain function.

The high-fat nature of the carnivore diet may also play a role in its potential benefits for mental health and cognitive function. The brain is composed of approximately 60% fat, and it relies on healthy fats for proper structure, function, and signaling. When you consume a diet rich in high-quality animal fats, such as those found in grass-fed beef, wild-caught fish, and pasture-raised eggs, you provide your brain with the building blocks it needs to function optimally.

In particular, the carnivore diet is rich in omega-3 fatty acids, which are essential for brain health. Omega-3s, particularly EPA and DHA, have been shown to support healthy brain development, improve mood and cognitive function, and reduce the risk of age-related cognitive decline. By incorporating fatty fish and other omega-3-rich animal products into your carnivore diet, you can help to ensure that your brain is getting the nutrients it needs to thrive.

Another way in which the carnivore diet may support mental health is through its ability to stabilize blood sugar levels. When you consume a diet high in carbohydrates, particularly refined and processed carbs, your blood sugar levels can experience significant fluctuations throughout the day. These fluctuations can lead to mood swings, irritability, and even symptoms of anxiety and depression. By eliminating carbohydrates and focusing on protein and fat, the carnivore diet can help to promote more stable blood sugar levels, which may translate to improved mood and cognitive function.

The carnivore diet's emphasis on high-quality protein may also have benefits for mental health and cognitive performance. Protein is essential for the production of neurotransmitters, the chemical messengers that transmit signals between brain cells and play a key role in regulating mood, motivation, and cognitive function. When you consume a diet rich in high-quality animal protein, you provide your body with the amino acids it needs to produce these important neurotransmitters, which may help to support optimal brain function and mental well-being.

In addition to its potential benefits for mood and cognitive function, the carnivore diet may also have implications for the treatment of certain mental health disorders. For example, some individuals with depression and anxiety have reported significant improvements in their symptoms after adopting a carnivore diet. While more research is needed to fully understand the mechanisms behind these potential benefits, it is thought that the diet's ability to reduce inflammation, stabilize blood sugar, and support neurotransmitter production may play a role.

It is important to note, however, that the carnivore diet is not a panacea for mental health issues, and it may not be appropriate or effective for everyone. As with any significant dietary change, it is essential to work closely with a qualified healthcare professional to ensure that the carnivore diet is safe and appropriate for your individual needs and goals. Additionally, if you are struggling with a mental health disorder, it is crucial to seek professional help and support, rather than relying solely on dietary changes to manage your symptoms.

That being said, for individuals who are interested in exploring the potential benefits of the carnivore diet for mental health and cognitive function, there are several strategies that can help to optimize results. One key approach is to focus on consuming a variety of high-quality animal products, including organ meats, which are particularly rich in nutrients that support brain health. Incorporating fermented animal products, such as kefir or fermented meats, may also help to support gut health and reduce inflammation, which can have positive implications for mental well-being.

Another important consideration is to pay attention to your individual response to the carnivore diet and make adjustments as needed. Some people may find that certain animal products, such as dairy or eggs, trigger digestive issues or other symptoms that can negatively impact mental health. By tuning into your body's signals and working with a healthcare professional to identify any potential sensitivities or intolerances, you can tailor your carnivore diet to best support your unique needs and goals.

The Carnivore Diet for Women's Health

The carnivore diet has emerged as a powerful tool for optimizing women's health, offering a unique approach to nourishing the female body and addressing common concerns. By focusing on nutrient-dense animal products and eliminating potentially problematic plant foods, women can experience profound improvements in their physical, mental, and emotional well-being. Let's delve into the specific benefits of the carnivore diet for women and explore how this way of eating can support their unique health needs.

One of the most significant advantages of the carnivore diet for women is its ability to regulate hormonal balance. Women's bodies are intricately connected to their hormonal rhythms, and imbalances can lead to a wide range of health issues, from menstrual irregularities and fertility challenges to mood swings and weight gain. The carnivore diet's emphasis on high-quality protein and healthy fats provides the building blocks for optimal hormone production and regulation. By consuming nutrient-dense animal products, such as grass-fed beef, wild-caught fish, and pasture-raised eggs, women can support the delicate interplay of estrogen, progesterone, and other key hormones that keep their bodies functioning at their best.

Moreover, the carnivore diet's elimination of common hormone-disrupting foods can further contribute to hormonal harmony. Many plant-based foods, such as soy, contain phytoestrogens, which can mimic the effects of estrogen in the body and throw off the natural balance. By removing these foods and focusing on clean, unprocessed animal products, women can create an internal environment that promotes optimal hormone function and minimizes the risk of hormone-related health issues.

The carnivore diet can also be a powerful ally in supporting women's reproductive health. For those struggling with fertility issues, the nutrient density of animal products can provide the essential building blocks for healthy ovulation, implantation, and fetal development. The high-quality protein, healthy fats, and key vitamins and minerals found in grass-fed meats, organ meats, and wild-caught fish can nourish the reproductive system and optimize fertility. Additionally, the absence of inflammatory plant compounds and antinutrients can reduce the burden on the body and allow it to allocate resources more effectively towards reproductive functions.

For women navigating the challenges of menopause, the carnivore diet offers a natural approach to managing symptoms and promoting overall well-being. The hormonal shifts that occur during menopause can lead to a range of discomforts, from hot flashes and night sweats to mood changes and sleep disturbances. By providing a stable source of energy and essential nutrients, the carnivore diet can help balance hormones, reduce inflammation, and support the body's natural transition through this life stage. The high-quality protein and healthy fats found in animal products can also help maintain lean muscle mass and bone density, which are crucial for women's health as they age.

Beyond its hormonal and reproductive benefits, the carnivore diet can also support women's mental and emotional well-being. The connection between gut health and brain function is well-established, and the carnivore diet's emphasis on easily digestible, nutrient-dense foods can promote a healthy gut microbiome. By eliminating potentially inflammatory plant compounds and focusing on bioavailable nutrients, women can support the production of neurotransmitters like serotonin and dopamine, which play crucial roles in mood regulation, stress management, and overall mental well-being.

Additionally, the simplicity and clarity of the carnivore diet can be mentally liberating for many women. In a world filled with conflicting dietary advice and constant pressure to conform to certain body ideals, the carnivore diet offers a refreshing break from the noise. By focusing on nourishing their bodies with high-quality animal products and listening to their own intuitive wisdom, women can cultivate a deeper sense of self-trust and body autonomy. This can be particularly empowering for those who have struggled with disordered eating patterns or body image issues in the past.

To maximize the benefits of the carnivore diet for women's health, it's essential to prioritize high-quality animal products and listen to your body's unique needs. Opt for grass-fed and pasture-raised meats, wild-caught fish, and organic eggs whenever possible, as these tend to have a more favorable nutrient profile and fewer contaminants. Pay attention to how different animal foods make you feel, and adjust your intake accordingly. Some women may thrive on a higher fat intake, while others may prefer leaner cuts of meat. Trust your body's wisdom and make adjustments as needed to optimize your individual health and well-being.

It's also important to approach the carnivore diet with a sense of self-compassion and flexibility. While the core principles of the diet involve focusing on animal products and eliminating plant foods, there may be times when small deviations feel necessary or appropriate. Whether it's incorporating a small amount of low-toxicity vegetables or enjoying a celebratory meal with loved ones, allow yourself the grace to make choices that align with your overall health goals and life circumstances. The carnivore diet is a powerful tool, but it's not a rigid set of rules that must be followed at all costs.

The Carnivore Diet for Men's Health

The Carnivore Diet has emerged as a powerful approach to optimizing men's health, offering a unique perspective on nutrition that challenges conventional wisdom. By focusing on nutrient-dense animal foods and eliminating potentially problematic plant-based ingredients, this way of eating has the potential to support hormonal balance, physical performance, and overall well-being. For men seeking to reclaim their vitality and unlock their full potential, the Carnivore Diet presents a compelling path to transformation.

At the core of the Carnivore Diet's benefits for men's health is its impact on hormone regulation. Testosterone, the primary male sex hormone, plays a crucial role in muscle growth, fat distribution, libido, and overall masculine characteristics. The high-fat, high-protein nature of the Carnivore Diet provides the building blocks necessary for optimal testosterone production. Saturated fats, in particular, have been shown to support healthy testosterone levels, and the Carnivore Diet is rich in these beneficial fats from sources like grass-fed beef, pasture-raised eggs, and wild-caught fish.

In addition to supporting testosterone production, the Carnivore Diet may also help reduce estrogen dominance, a condition characterized by an imbalance between estrogen and progesterone levels. Excessive estrogen in men can lead to a host of health issues, including gynecomastia (enlarged breast tissue), decreased libido, and mood disturbances. By eliminating estrogenic foods like soy, flax, and certain plastics, the Carnivore Diet can help restore hormonal balance and promote a more favorable estrogen-to-testosterone ratio.

The high-protein nature of the Carnivore Diet is another key factor in its potential to support men's health. Protein is essential for building and maintaining lean muscle mass, which is critical for physical performance, metabolic health, and overall vitality. Animal proteins, such as those found in meat, eggs, and fish, are considered complete proteins, meaning they contain all the essential amino acids needed for optimal muscle protein synthesis. Consuming adequate protein on the Carnivore Diet can help preserve and enhance muscle mass, even as men age.

The Carnivore Diet's emphasis on nutrient density is also particularly beneficial for men's health. Many animal foods are rich in vitamins and minerals that are crucial for male vitality, such as zinc, selenium, and vitamin D. Zinc, for example, is essential for testosterone production, immune function, and prostate health. Oysters, beef, and lamb are all excellent sources of zinc, making them valuable additions to a Carnivore Diet protocol. Selenium, found in abundance in Brazil nuts, sardines, and grass-fed beef, is another important mineral for men's health, supporting thyroid function and acting as a potent antioxidant.

Vitamin D, often referred to as the "sunshine vitamin," is another critical nutrient for men's health that is well-represented in the Carnivore Diet. This fat-soluble vitamin plays a role in testosterone production, bone health, and immune function. While sunlight exposure is the best way to obtain vitamin D, certain animal foods like fatty fish, egg yolks, and liver also contain significant amounts. Incorporating these vitamin D-rich foods into a Carnivore Diet protocol can help ensure optimal levels of this essential nutrient.

The Carnivore Diet's potential to reduce inflammation is another aspect that makes it appealing for men's health. Chronic inflammation has been linked to a wide range of health issues, including heart disease, diabetes, and certain cancers. By eliminating potentially inflammatory foods like refined carbohydrates, processed oils, and certain plant compounds, the Carnivore Diet may help reduce systemic inflammation and promote overall health. The high intake of omega-3 fatty acids from sources like wild-caught fish and grass-fed beef can also contribute to an anti-inflammatory effect.

Digestive health is another area where the Carnivore Diet may offer benefits for men. Many plant foods contain lectins, phytates, and other antinutrients that can interfere with nutrient absorption and contribute to digestive distress. By eliminating these potentially problematic compounds, the Carnivore Diet can help improve gut health and reduce symptoms like bloating, gas, and indigestion. The high-fat nature of the diet also supports the production of bile acids, which are essential for proper digestion and absorption of nutrients.

While the Carnivore Diet offers numerous potential benefits for men's health, it's important to approach this way of eating with care and consideration. Transitioning to a meat-based diet can be a significant change for some, and it may take time for the body to adapt. Start gradually, perhaps by eliminating one food group at a time, and pay attention to how your body responds. Some men may experience temporary digestive discomfort or flu-like symptoms during the adaptation phase, but these often subside as the body adjusts to the new way of eating.

It's also crucial to prioritize high-quality animal products when following a Carnivore Diet. Choose grass-fed and pasture-raised meats, wild-caught fish, and organic eggs whenever possible. These options tend to have a more favorable nutrient profile and are less likely to contain harmful additives or contaminants. Incorporating a variety of animal foods, including organ meats, can also help ensure a comprehensive intake of essential nutrients.

As with any dietary approach, it's important to consult with a qualified healthcare professional before making significant changes to your eating habits. While the Carnivore Diet can be a powerful tool for optimizing men's health, it may not be suitable for everyone. Those with pre-existing health conditions, such as kidney disease or certain metabolic disorders, should exercise caution and seek personalized guidance from a medical expert.

CHAPTER 5

LONG-TERM SUCCESS ON THE CARNIVORE DIET

Maintaining Results and Preventing Relapses

Embracing the carnivore diet is not just a temporary fix, but a long-term commitment to a healthier, more vibrant life. As you begin to experience the many benefits of this way of eating, such as increased energy, improved digestion, and better overall health, it's crucial to develop strategies for maintaining your results and preventing relapses. By establishing a strong foundation of healthy habits, cultivating a supportive mindset, and staying connected to your reasons for choosing this path, you can ensure that your success on the carnivore diet is not just a fleeting victory, but a lifelong transformation.

One of the most important aspects of maintaining your results on the carnivore diet is consistency. Just as it took time and dedication to adapt to this new way of eating and start seeing benefits, it will require ongoing effort and commitment to sustain your progress. Make the carnivore diet a non-negotiable part of your daily routine, prioritizing high-quality animal products and staying true to the core principles of the diet. Plan your meals in advance, keep your kitchen stocked with nutrient-dense options, and make sure you always have carnivore-friendly snacks on hand for those moments when hunger strikes or temptation arises.

Developing a strong support system is another key factor in maintaining your success on the carnivore diet. Surround yourself with like-minded individuals who share your commitment to health and well-being, whether that means joining online communities, attending local meetups, or enlisting the support of friends and family members. Having people to turn to for encouragement, advice, and accountability can make all the difference when you're facing challenges or feeling discouraged. Don't be afraid to reach out for help when you need it, and remember that you're not alone in this journey.

Mindset is another critical component of long-term success on the carnivore diet. Cultivate a positive, growth-oriented outlook, focusing on the incredible benefits you've experienced and the progress you've made rather than dwelling on any temporary setbacks or challenges. Celebrate your victories, no matter how small, and use them as motivation to keep pushing forward. When you do encounter obstacles or temptations, remember your reasons for choosing this path and reconnect with your deeper purpose. Whether your goal is to heal from chronic illness, optimize your physical performance, or simply feel your best, keeping your "why" front and center can help you stay committed and motivated.

It's also essential to be proactive in identifying and addressing any potential triggers or risk factors for relapse. Pay attention to your emotional state, stress levels, and sleep patterns, as these can all impact your ability to stick with the carnivore diet and maintain your results. Develop healthy coping mechanisms for managing stress, such as meditation, deep breathing, or gentle exercise, and make sure you're prioritizing quality sleep each night. If you find yourself slipping into old habits or craving non-carnivore foods, take a step back and assess what might be driving those urges. Are you feeling bored, anxious, or deprived? Address the underlying issues head-on, and develop strategies for navigating those challenges in a way that aligns with your goals and values.

Another powerful tool for maintaining your results on the carnivore diet is continual education and experimentation. Stay curious and open-minded, seeking out new information and perspectives on this way of eating. Read books and articles, listen to podcasts, and engage with experts in the field to deepen your understanding of the science and principles behind the carnivore diet. At the same time, be willing to experiment with different approaches and techniques to find what works best for your unique body and lifestyle. Whether that means trying new recipes, experimenting with intermittent fasting, or incorporating specific nutrient-dense foods like organ meats, staying engaged and proactive in your carnivore journey can help you continue to thrive and grow.

Cyclical Carnivore Dieting and Reintroducing Foods

Cyclical carnivore dieting, also known as the "carnivore cycle" or "carnivore reset," is an approach that involves alternating periods of strict carnivore eating with the strategic reintroduction of selected plant foods. This method can be particularly useful for individuals who have experienced benefits from the carnivore diet but wish to expand their food choices or address specific nutrient needs. By carefully reintroducing foods and monitoring your body's response, you can create a personalized dietary approach that supports your health goals while still maintaining the core principles of the carnivore way of eating.

The first step in implementing a cyclical carnivore diet is to establish a baseline period of strict carnivore eating. During this time, which typically lasts anywhere from a few weeks to several months, you will consume only animal products, such as meat, fish, eggs, and dairy (if tolerated). This initial phase allows your body to adapt to the carnivore diet, heal from any potential food sensitivities or intolerances, and establish a foundation of nutrient-dense eating. It is important to pay close attention to your body during this time, noting any changes in energy levels, digestion, mental clarity, and overall well-being.

Once you have completed the baseline phase and feel stable on the carnivore diet, you can begin the process of strategically reintroducing plant foods. It is crucial to approach this process slowly and methodically, introducing one food at a time and monitoring your body's response. Start by choosing a single plant food that you wish to reintroduce, such as a low-toxicity vegetable like leafy greens or a small portion of a starchy tuber like sweet potato. Consume this food in isolation, without any other new additions to your diet, for a period of three to five days.

During the reintroduction phase, keep a detailed food and symptom journal to track your body's response to the newly introduced food. Pay attention to any changes in digestion, energy levels, skin health, joint pain, or other symptoms that may indicate a sensitivity or intolerance. If you do not notice any adverse reactions after the initial reintroduction period, you can consider incorporating that food into your regular diet in moderation. However, if you experience negative symptoms, it is best to remove the food from your diet and allow your body time to recover before attempting to reintroduce another food.

As you continue the process of reintroducing plant foods, it is important to prioritize nutrient-dense options that offer specific benefits for your health goals. Some examples of nutrient-dense plant foods that may be well-tolerated on a cyclical carnivore diet include:

- Low-toxicity vegetables: Leafy greens, cucumber, celery, and summer squash
- Low-sugar fruits: Berries, avocado, and olives

- Starchy tubers: Sweet potato, cassava, and yuca

- Fermented vegetables: Sauerkraut, kimchi, and pickles

- Nuts and seeds: Macadamia nuts, brazil nuts, and pumpkin seeds

When reintroducing these foods, be mindful of portion sizes and frequency of consumption. Some individuals may find that they tolerate small amounts of certain plant foods well, while others may need to limit their intake or consume them only occasionally. The key is to find a balance that works for your unique body and health needs.

One potential benefit of cyclical carnivore dieting is the ability to address specific nutrient needs or health concerns that may not be fully met on a strict carnivore diet. For example, some individuals may require additional fiber for digestive health, while others may benefit from the antioxidants and phytochemicals found in certain plant foods. By strategically incorporating these foods into your diet, you can support your overall health while still maintaining the core principles of the carnivore approach.

Another advantage of the cyclical approach is the flexibility it offers for social situations and travel. Strict carnivore dieting can be challenging to maintain in certain settings, such as dining out with friends or attending family gatherings. By allowing for the occasional inclusion of selected plant foods, you can navigate these situations more easily and reduce the stress associated with adhering to a rigid dietary protocol.

It is important to note that the cyclical carnivore approach may not be suitable for everyone, and individual responses to reintroduced foods will vary. Some people may find that they thrive on a strict carnivore diet and do not tolerate the reintroduction of plant foods well. Others may discover that they can include a wider variety of plant foods without experiencing negative symptoms. It is crucial to listen to your body and adjust your approach based on your unique needs and goals.

If you are considering a cyclical carnivore approach, it is always best to consult with a healthcare professional who is knowledgeable about the carnivore diet and can provide personalized guidance. They can help you assess your individual nutrient needs, monitor your progress, and address any potential concerns that may arise during the reintroduction process.

The Carnivore Diet as a Lifestyle: Mindset and Sustainability

Adopting the carnivore diet is not just a temporary change in eating habits, but rather a long-term commitment to a new way of life. To truly thrive on this unconventional way of eating, it is essential to cultivate a mindset that supports sustainability and resilience in the face of challenges. In this chapter, we will explore the importance of developing a carnivore lifestyle mindset and provide practical strategies for making this way of eating a sustainable and enjoyable part of your life.

One of the key elements of a successful carnivore lifestyle is a strong sense of purpose and motivation. It is important to have a clear understanding of why you have chosen to adopt this way of eating, whether it be for improved health, increased energy, or a desire to simplify your relationship with food. By connecting with your deeper reasons for pursuing the carnivore diet, you can cultivate a sense of intrinsic motivation that will help you stay committed and focused even when faced with obstacles or temptations.

Another crucial aspect of a carnivore lifestyle mindset is a willingness to experiment and adapt. While the core principles of the carnivore diet are relatively simple - consume animal products and eliminate plant-based foods - there is still significant room for individual variation and customization. Some people may thrive on a diet composed primarily of beef, while others may find that they feel best when incorporating a wider variety of animal products, such as pork, lamb, or fish. By approaching the carnivore diet with a spirit of curiosity and openness, you can discover the specific foods and eating patterns that work best for your unique needs and preferences.

Cultivating a growth mindset is also essential for long-term success on the carnivore diet. Rather than viewing challenges or setbacks as failures, try to see them as opportunities for learning and growth. If you find yourself struggling with cravings or experiencing digestive issues, take a proactive approach to problem-solving and seek out resources and support to help you navigate these challenges. By embracing a growth mindset, you can develop greater resilience and adaptability in the face of the inevitable ups and downs of the carnivore lifestyle.

One practical strategy for supporting a sustainable carnivore lifestyle is to focus on building strong habits and routines around food preparation and meal planning. By taking the time to source high-quality animal products, create a variety of delicious and satisfying meals, and establish a regular eating schedule, you can make the carnivore diet a more seamless and enjoyable part of your daily life. Consider batch-cooking larger portions of meat or making use of a slow cooker or pressure cooker to streamline meal preparation and ensure that you always have nourishing carnivore options on hand.

Another key strategy for maintaining a sustainable carnivore lifestyle is to cultivate a strong support system. Surround yourself with people who understand and respect your dietary choices, whether that means connecting with other carnivore dieters online or seeking out like-minded friends and family members in your local community. Having a network of supportive and encouraging individuals can provide a valuable source of motivation, accountability, and inspiration as you navigate the challenges and triumphs of the carnivore lifestyle.

It is also important to practice self-compassion and flexibility as you adopt the carnivore diet. Remember that perfection is not the goal, and that it is okay to have occasional slip-ups or indulgences. What matters most is your overall commitment to nourishing your body with high-quality animal products and prioritizing your health and well-being. By approaching the carnivore diet with a sense of balance and self-kindness, you can avoid the trap of rigidity or self-judgment and instead focus on making sustainable, long-term progress.

In addition to cultivating a supportive mindset and strong habits, it can also be helpful to find ways to make the carnivore lifestyle more enjoyable and satisfying. Take the time to explore new recipes and cooking techniques, and don't be afraid to get creative with your meal choices. Experiment with different cuts of meat, try new seasonings and flavor profiles, and find ways to make your carnivore meals a source of pleasure and satisfaction. By focusing on the delicious and nourishing aspects of the carnivore diet, you can help to reinforce your commitment to this way of eating and make it a more sustainable part of your life.

Another important consideration for long-term success on the carnivore diet is to prioritize self-care and stress management. While the carnivore diet can have powerful benefits for physical and mental health, it is not a cure-all for the stresses and challenges of daily life. Make sure to carve out time for activities that help you relax and recharge, whether that means engaging in regular exercise, practicing meditation or deep breathing, or pursuing hobbies and interests that bring you joy and fulfillment. By taking a holistic approach to your well-being and prioritizing both your physical and emotional needs, you can create a strong foundation for a sustainable and thriving carnivore lifestyle.

Building a Support Network and Finding Community

Embarking on the carnivore diet can be a transformative journey, but it's one that is best undertaken with the support and encouragement of others who share your goals and values. Building a strong network of like-minded individuals and finding a sense of community can make all the difference in your success and overall experience with this way of eating. Let's explore the importance of cultivating a supportive environment and offer practical strategies for connecting with others on a similar path.

One of the most significant benefits of building a support network is the sense of camaraderie and shared purpose it provides. When you surround yourself with others who are also committed to the carnivore lifestyle, you create a positive feedback loop of motivation, accountability, and inspiration. Knowing that you're not alone in your journey can be incredibly empowering, especially during times when you may face challenges or doubts. Having a community to lean on can provide the encouragement and guidance you need to stay the course and maintain your commitment to optimal health.

Moreover, connecting with others who follow the carnivore diet can be a valuable source of knowledge and practical advice. As you navigate this new way of eating, you're bound to have questions, concerns, and moments of uncertainty. By tapping into the collective wisdom of your support network, you can gain insights, tips, and strategies that can help you overcome obstacles and optimize your approach. Whether it's learning about the best sources of high-quality animal products, discovering new recipe ideas, or troubleshooting common challenges, your community can be an invaluable resource for growth and learning.

So, how can you go about building a support network and finding your carnivore community? One of the most accessible and effective ways is to leverage the power of online platforms and social media. There are numerous Facebook groups, Reddit communities, and Instagram accounts dedicated to the carnivore diet, where individuals from all walks of life come together to share their experiences, ask questions, and offer support. By joining these virtual spaces, you can connect with others who are on a similar journey, learn from their successes and challenges, and feel a sense of belonging within a larger movement.

When engaging with online communities, it's essential to approach the process with an open mind and a willingness to learn. Remember that everyone's journey is unique, and what works for one person may not necessarily work for another. Be respectful of different perspectives and experiences, and focus on building genuine connections based on shared values and goals. Over time, you may find that you develop deeper relationships with certain individuals within these communities, forming friendships that extend beyond the virtual realm and into your offline life.

In addition to online communities, seeking out local connections can be incredibly valuable in building a strong support network. Look for opportunities to attend events, workshops, or meetups related to the carnivore diet or ancestral health in your area. These gatherings can be fantastic ways to meet like-minded individuals in person, share stories and insights, and forge meaningful connections. You may even consider starting your own local group or hosting events to bring together others who share your passion for the carnivore lifestyle.

Another powerful way to find support and community is to enlist the help of a mentor or coach who specializes in the carnivore diet. Having a knowledgeable guide who can offer personalized advice, answer your questions, and provide accountability can be invaluable in navigating the ups and downs of your journey. Many experienced carnivore practitioners offer coaching services, either in-person or remotely, and can help you optimize your approach, overcome challenges, and stay motivated along the way. By investing in a mentorship relationship, you not only gain access to expert guidance but also become part of a larger community of individuals committed to thriving on the carnivore diet.

As you build your support network and find your carnivore community, it's important to remember that the connections you forge can extend far beyond the realm of diet and nutrition. Many people who adopt the carnivore lifestyle find that it becomes a catalyst for profound personal growth and transformation. By surrounding yourself with others who share your values and aspirations, you create opportunities for deeper connections, meaningful conversations, and shared experiences that enrich your life in countless ways.

Ultimately, building a strong support network and finding a sense of community is an essential part of thriving on the carnivore diet. By leveraging online platforms, seeking out local connections, and investing in mentorship relationships, you can create a powerful ecosystem of support, encouragement, and shared wisdom. As you navigate this transformative journey, remember that you are part of a larger movement of individuals committed to optimal health, vitality, and personal growth. Embrace the power of community, and let it fuel your success and fulfillment on the carnivore path.

Addressing Social Situations and Eating Out on the Carnivore Diet

Navigating social situations and dining out can be one of the most challenging aspects of following the Carnivore Diet. In a world where plant-based foods dominate menus and social gatherings, sticking to a meat-only approach can feel isolating and restrictive. However, with a bit of preparation, flexibility, and communication, it's entirely possible to enjoy a thriving social life while remaining committed to your dietary principles. By developing strategies for eating out, hosting events, and communicating your needs, you can find a balance that allows you to prioritize your health without compromising your relationships or social experiences.

One of the keys to successfully navigating social situations on the Carnivore Diet is to plan ahead. Before attending a gathering or eating out, take some time to research the menu options and identify any carnivore-friendly dishes. Many restaurants offer steak, burger patties without the bun, grilled chicken, or seafood options that can easily be adapted to fit your dietary needs. Don't be afraid to ask questions about the ingredients and preparation methods, and request modifications where necessary. Most establishments are happy to accommodate special dietary requests, especially if you communicate your needs politely and clearly.

When dining out, focus on the simplest options available. A plain steak or burger patty with no seasoning or sauce is often the safest choice, as it minimizes the risk of hidden ingredients or cross-contamination. If you're unsure about the quality of the meat or cooking oils used, consider bringing your own small container of grass-fed butter or ghee to add flavor and ensure you're consuming healthy fats. Avoid dishes that come with breading, sauces, or complex seasonings, as these may contain non-carnivore ingredients like flour, sugar, or vegetable oils.

In situations where suitable options are limited, such as at a cocktail party or a friend's home, it's helpful to have a few go-to strategies in mind. One approach is to eat a satisfying carnivore meal before the event, so you're not relying on the available food to meet your nutritional needs. This can help reduce the temptation to stray from your dietary principles and make it easier to navigate the social aspects of the gathering without feeling deprived or hungry.

Another strategy is to offer to bring a dish to share that aligns with your Carnivore Diet principles. This not only ensures that you'll have something suitable to eat but also provides an opportunity to introduce others to the delicious possibilities of a meat-based approach. Consider preparing a charcuterie board with high-quality cured meats, pâté, and cheese (if you include dairy), or a platter of grilled steak bites with a carnivore-friendly dipping sauce like herb butter or chimichurri (sans the typical non-carnivore ingredients).

When hosting your own social gatherings, you have the advantage of being able to control the menu and create a carnivore-friendly spread. Focus on high-quality, well-sourced meats and simple preparation methods that showcase the natural flavors of the ingredients. A backyard barbecue with grass-fed burgers, grilled steaks, and chicken wings can be a crowd-pleaser, while still allowing you to stay true to your dietary principles. If you're hosting a sit-down dinner, consider a theme like "Steak Night" or "Surf and Turf" to keep the focus on carnivore-friendly options.

It's important to remember that the Carnivore Diet is a personal choice, and not everyone will understand or support your decision to follow this way of eating. Some people may express concern, skepticism, or even criticism when they learn about your dietary approach. In these situations, it's essential to communicate your motivations and experiences clearly and confidently, without feeling the need to justify or defend your choices. Share your personal success stories, the health benefits you've experienced, and the research that supports the potential advantages of a carnivore approach.

At the same time, it's crucial to be respectful of others' dietary choices and preferences. Just as you want your decisions to be respected, it's important to extend the same courtesy to those who follow different eating patterns. Avoid engaging in debates or trying to convert others to your way of thinking, and instead focus on finding common ground and enjoying the social aspects of the gathering.

If you find that your dietary choices are causing significant strain on your relationships or social interactions, it may be worth considering a more flexible approach in certain situations. While the ideal scenario is to maintain a strict Carnivore Diet, there may be times when a bit of compromise is necessary for the sake of social harmony. This could mean allowing yourself a small deviation from your usual protocol, such as enjoying a piece of dark chocolate or a glass of red wine on a special occasion, or simply focusing on the main meat dish while politely passing on the non-carnivore sides.

Ultimately, the key to successfully navigating social situations and eating out on the Carnivore Diet is to find a balance that works for you. By planning ahead, communicating your needs, and being open to flexibility when necessary, you can maintain your commitment to your health goals without sacrificing your social connections or enjoyment of life. Remember that the Carnivore Diet is a tool for optimizing your well-being, not a rigid set of rules that should dominate every aspect of your existence.

As you become more comfortable and confident in your carnivore lifestyle, you may find that social situations become easier to navigate. You'll develop a repertoire of go-to strategies, learn to communicate your needs more effectively, and find a supportive network of like-minded individuals who understand and respect your choices. By approaching social situations with a positive attitude, a willingness to adapt, and a commitment to your health, you can thrive on the Carnivore Diet while still enjoying a rich and fulfilling social life.

CHAPTER 6

CARNIVORE DIET RECIPES AND MEAL IDEAS

Breakfast Recipes

Classic Steak and Eggs

Prep Time: 5 mins

Cook Time: 10 mins

Total Time: 15 mins

Ingredients:

- 2 large eggs
- 1 ribeye steak (8 oz)
- Salt and pepper to taste
- 1 tbsp butter or ghee

Preparation:

- Season the steak with salt and pepper.
- Heat a skillet over medium-high heat and add butter or ghee.
- Cook the steak for 4-5 minutes per side for medium-rare, or to your desired level of doneness.
- Remove the steak and let it rest.
- In the same skillet, reduce heat to medium and cook the eggs to your preference (scrambled, over-easy, etc.).
- Serve the steak with eggs on the side.

---

2. Bacon-Wrapped Asparagus

Prep Time: 5 mins

Cook Time: 20 mins

Ingredients:

- 8 asparagus spears
- 8 slices of bacon

Preparation:

- Preheat your oven to 400°F (200°C).
- Wrap each asparagus spear with a slice of bacon.

- Place on a baking sheet lined with parchment paper.
- Bake for 20 minutes or until the bacon is crispy.
- Serve hot as a protein-packed breakfast side.

---

3. Carnivore Omelette

Prep Time: 5 mins

Cook Time: 8 mins

Ingredients:

- 3 large eggs
- 1 tbsp butter or ghee
- 1/2 cup cooked shredded chicken
- Salt to taste

Preparation:

- Beat the eggs with salt.
- Heat butter in a non-stick skillet over medium heat.
- Pour in the eggs and cook until they begin to set on the bottom.
- Sprinkle shredded chicken over half of the omelette.
- Fold the omelette in half over the filling and continue to cook until the eggs are set.
- Slide onto a plate and serve.

---

4. Pork Belly Strips

Prep Time: 5 mins

Cook Time: 30 mins

Ingredients:

- 1 lb pork belly strips
- Salt and pepper to taste

Preparation:

- Preheat the oven to 400°F (200°C).
- Season the pork belly strips with salt and pepper.
- Place them on a wire rack over a baking tray.
- Bake for 30 minutes or until crispy.

- Serve hot.

---

5. Carnivore Scotch Eggs

Prep Time: 10 mins

Cook Time: 25 mins

Ingredients:

- 4 hard-boiled eggs, peeled
- 1 lb ground pork or sausage meat
- Salt and pepper to taste

Preparation:

- Preheat your oven to 350°F (175°C).
- Season the ground pork with salt and pepper.
- Flatten the ground pork and wrap each egg with the meat until fully enclosed.
- Place the meat-wrapped eggs on a baking sheet.
- Bake for 25 minutes or until the meat is cooked through.
- Serve warm or at room temperature.

---

6. Beef Liver with Onions

Prep Time: 10 mins

Cook Time: 10 mins

Ingredients:

- 1 lb beef liver, thinly sliced
- 1 large onion, thinly sliced (optional for strict carnivore)
- Salt and pepper to taste
- 2 tbsp butter or ghee

Preparation:

- Season the liver slices with salt and pepper.
- Heat butter in a large skillet over medium heat.
- Add the onion and cook until softened if using; otherwise, skip to step 4.
- Increase heat to high, add liver slices, and cook quickly for about 2 minutes per side.
- Serve hot, with onions if included.

7. Carnivore Pancakes

Prep Time: 5 mins

Cook Time: 10 mins

Ingredients:

- 4 oz cream cheese
- 6 large eggs
- Butter for frying

Preparation:

- Blend cream cheese and eggs together until smooth.
- Heat butter in a non-stick skillet over medium heat.
- Pour small amounts of the batter into the skillet to form pancakes.
- Cook until golden on one side, then flip and cook the other side.
- Serve hot.

8. Chicken Thighs with Crispy Skin

Prep Time: 5 mins

Cook Time: 35 mins

Ingredients:

- 4 chicken thighs, bone-in and skin-on
- Salt to taste

Preparation:

- Preheat oven to 400°F (200°C).
- Pat the chicken thighs dry with paper towels and season with salt.
- Place them skin-side up on a baking sheet or oven-proof skillet.
- Bake for 35 minutes or until the skin is crispy and the chicken is cooked through.
- Serve hot with the crispy skin.

9. Carnivore Diet Burger Patties

Prep Time: 5 mins

Cook Time: 10 mins

Ingredients:

- 1 lb ground beef (80/20)
- Salt to taste

Preparation:

- Preheat your grill or skillet over medium-high heat.
- Form the ground beef into patties and season with salt on both sides.
- Grill or cook the patties for about 5 minutes per side for medium-rare.
- Remove from heat and let rest for a couple of minutes.
- Serve the patties as is, or with a side of fried eggs.

10. Butter-Basted Ribeye

Prep Time: 5 mins

Cook Time: 10 mins

Ingredients:

- 1 ribeye steak (8 oz)
- 2 tbsp butter
- Salt to taste

Preparation:

- Heat a heavy skillet over high heat and add the steak, seasoned with salt.
- Cook the steak for about 3 minutes on one side, then flip.
- Add butter to the skillet and baste the steak with the melted butter for another 3 minutes.
- Continue to cook to your desired level of doneness, basting frequently.
- Rest the steak for a few minutes before serving.

11. Carnivore Breakfast Sausages

Prep Time: 10 mins

Cook Time: 10 mins

Ingredients:

- 1 lb ground pork
- 1 tsp salt
- 1/2 tsp black pepper

- 1/2 tsp sage (optional)

Preparation:

- Mix the ground pork with salt, pepper, and sage (if using) in a bowl.
- Form the mixture into small patties.
- Cook the patties in a skillet over medium heat for about 5 minutes per side or until cooked through.
- Serve hot as a breakfast side.

---

12. Carnivore Diet Bone Marrow

Prep Time: 5 mins

Cook Time: 20 mins

Ingredients:

- 4 beef marrow bones, cut lengthwise
- Salt to taste

Preparation:

- Preheat oven to 450°F (230°C).
- Place marrow bones on a baking sheet, salt the marrow, and roast for 20 minutes.
- Scoop out the marrow and serve hot, optionally with a sprinkle of salt.

---

13. Crustless Carnivore Quiche

Prep Time: 10 mins

Cook Time: 35 mins

Ingredients:

- 6 large eggs
- 1 cup heavy cream
- 1 cup cooked and crumbled bacon
- 1 cup grated cheese (optional for strict carnivore)
- Salt to taste

Preparation:

- Preheat oven to 350°F (175°C).
- Whisk together eggs, heavy cream, and salt.
- Stir in the bacon and cheese if using.

- Pour the mixture into a greased pie dish.
- Bake for 35 minutes or until the quiche is set and the top is golden brown.
- Let cool slightly before serving.

---

14. Carnivore Diet "Bread" Loaf

Prep Time: 10 mins

Cook Time: 30 mins

Ingredients:

- 10 egg whites
- 1 cup powdered parmesan cheese (optional for strict carnivore)

Preparation:

- Preheat oven to 325°F (165°C).
- Beat the egg whites until stiff peaks form.
- Gently fold in the powdered parmesan cheese if using.
- Pour into a greased loaf pan and bake for 30 minutes or until golden.
- Cool before slicing.

---

15. Carnivore Breakfast Skewers

Prep Time: 10 mins

Cook Time: 10 mins

Ingredients:

- 1 lb steak, cut into cubes
- 1 lb chicken breasts, cut into cubes
- Salt to taste

Preparation:

- Preheat your grill to medium-high heat.
- Season the meat cubes with salt.
- Thread the steak and chicken cubes onto skewers, alternating between the two.
- Grill the skewers for about 4-5 minutes on each side or until the meat is cooked to your liking.
- Remove from the grill and serve hot.

---

16. Carnivore Diet Breakfast Bowls

Prep Time: 5 mins

Cook Time: 15 mins

Ingredients:

- 4 large eggs
- 1/2 lb ground beef
- Salt to taste

Preparation:

- Cook the ground beef in a skillet over medium heat until fully browned. Season with salt and set aside.
- In the same skillet, fry the eggs to your desired doneness.
- Divide the cooked ground beef into bowls and top each with a fried egg.
- Serve immediately.

---

17. Carnivore Diet Ham Rolls

Prep Time: 5 mins

Cook Time: 0 mins

Ingredients:

- Slices of deli ham
- Cream cheese (optional for strict carnivore)

Preparation:

- Lay out the ham slices.
- Spread a thin layer of cream cheese on each slice if using.
- Roll up the ham slices and secure with toothpicks if necessary.
- Serve as a quick and easy breakfast option.

---

18. Carnivore Diet Fish Breakfast

Prep Time: 5 mins

Cook Time: 10 mins

Ingredients:

- 2 (6 oz) fish fillets, such as salmon or cod
- Salt to taste

- 1 tbsp butter or ghee

Preparation:

- Season the fish fillets with salt.
- Heat butter in a skillet over medium-high heat.
- Add the fish fillets skin-side down and cook for about 5 minutes.
- Flip the fillets and cook for an additional 4-5 minutes or until cooked through.
- Serve immediately.

---

19. Carnivore Diet Breakfast Tacos

Prep Time: 5 mins

Cook Time: 10 mins

Ingredients:

- 4 large eggs
- 4 slices of cheese (such as cheddar or provolone)
- Salt to taste

Preparation:

- Cook the eggs in a non-stick skillet as you would for an omelet, seasoning with salt.
- Once the eggs are almost set, place a slice of cheese on one half and fold the other half over to create a taco shape.
- Press gently and cook until the cheese begins to melt.
- Serve immediately as a handheld breakfast.

---

20. Carnivore Breakfast Meatballs

Prep Time: 10 mins

Cook Time: 20 mins

Ingredients:

- 1 lb ground meat (beef, pork, or a mix)
- 1/2 tsp salt
- 1/4 tsp black pepper
- 1/4 tsp garlic powder (optional for strict carnivore)

Preparation:

- Preheat your oven to 400°F (200°C).

- Mix the ground meat with salt, pepper, and garlic powder if using.
- Form the mixture into small balls and place them on a baking sheet.
- Bake for 20 minutes or until the meatballs are browned and cooked through.
- Serve hot, perhaps with a side of fried or scrambled eggs.

Lunch Recipes

1. Classic Steak Lunch

Prep Time: 5 mins

Cook Time: 10 mins

Ingredients:

- 1 ribeye steak (or your preferred cut)
- Salt
- Black pepper (optional)

Preparation:

- Season the steak generously with salt and pepper if using.
- Preheat a skillet over high heat and cook the steak to your preferred level of doneness.
- Let the steak rest for a few minutes before slicing. Serve.

---

2. Chicken Thighs with Crispy Skin

Prep Time: 5 mins

Cook Time: 25 mins

Ingredients:

- 4 chicken thighs, skin-on
- Salt

Preparation:

- Preheat your oven to 400°F (200°C).
- Season chicken thighs with salt.
- Place them skin-side down in a cold non-stick skillet and turn the heat to medium-high.
- Cook until the skin is crispy, then flip and transfer the skillet to the oven.
- Bake until the chicken is cooked through. Serve.

---

3. Seared Salmon Fillets

Prep Time: 5 mins

Cook Time: 10 mins

Ingredients:

- 2 salmon fillets
- Salt

Preparation:

- Season the salmon fillets with salt.
- Heat a non-stick skillet over medium-high heat and place the salmon skin-side down.
- Cook until the skin is crispy, then flip and finish cooking until desired doneness. Serve.

4. Pork Chop with Butter

Prep Time: 5 mins

Cook Time: 12 mins

Ingredients:

- 2 pork chops, bone-in
- Salt
- Butter

Preparation:

- Season the pork chops with salt.
- Heat a skillet over medium-high heat and add a knob of butter.
- Sear the pork chops until golden and cooked to your liking. Serve with a dollop of butter.

5. Beef Liver with Onions

Prep Time: 10 mins

Cook Time: 10 mins

Ingredients:

- 1 lb beef liver, sliced
- 1 onion, sliced (optional for strict carnivore)
- Salt

Preparation:

- Season the liver slices with salt.
- In a skillet over medium heat, cook the onions until soft and set aside (if using).
- In the same skillet, cook the liver for about 3 minutes per side. Serve with onions on top.

---

6. Lamb Rack Roast

Prep Time: 5 mins

Cook Time: 25 mins

Ingredients:

- 1 rack of lamb
- Salt
- Rosemary (optional)

Preparation:

- Preheat your oven to 400°F (200°C).
- Season the lamb rack with salt and rosemary if using.
- Roast in the oven until the meat reaches your preferred level of doneness. Serve.

---

7. Carnivore Diet Burger Patties

Prep Time: 5 mins

Cook Time: 10 mins

Ingredients:

- 1 lb ground beef
- Salt

Preparation:

- Form the beef into patties and season with salt.
- Cook in a skillet over medium-high heat to your preferred level of doneness. Serve.

---

8. Grilled Ribeye Cap

Prep Time: 5 mins

Cook Time: 10 mins

Ingredients:

- Ribeye cap steak

- Salt

Preparation:

- Season the ribeye cap with salt.

- Grill over high heat to your desired level of doneness. Serve.

---

9. Bacon-Wrapped Chicken Breasts

Prep Time: 10 mins

Cook Time: 25 mins

Ingredients:

- 4 chicken breasts

- 8 slices of bacon

- Salt

Preparation:

- Preheat your oven to 375°F (190°C).

- Season the chicken breasts with salt.

- Wrap each breast with two slices of bacon.

- Bake until the chicken is cooked through and the bacon is crispy. Serve.

---

10. Sizzling Butter Shrimp

Prep Time: 5 mins

Cook Time: 5 mins

Ingredients:

- 1 lb shrimp, peeled anddeveined

- Salt

- Butter

Preparation:

- Season the shrimp with salt.

- Heat a generous amount of butter in a skillet over medium-high heat.

- Add shrimp and cook until pink and opaque. Serve immediately.

---

11. Quick Seared Scallops

Prep Time: 5 mins

Cook Time: 4 mins

Ingredients:

- 1 lb scallops
- Salt
- Butter

Preparation:

- Pat scallops dry and season with salt.
- In a skillet, heat butter over high heat until frothy.
- Sear scallops for about 2 minutes per side until golden brown and cooked through. Serve.

---

12. Beef Short Ribs

Prep Time: 5 mins

Cook Time: 3 hrs

Ingredients:

- 2 lbs beef short ribs
- Salt

Preparation:

- Preheat your oven to 300°F (150°C).
- Season the ribs generously with salt.
- Place in a roasting pan and cover with foil.
- Roast for about 3 hours or until meat is tender. Serve.

---

13. Carnivore Diet Meatza

Prep Time: 10 mins

Cook Time: 15 mins

Ingredients:

- 1 lb ground meat (beef, chicken, or pork)
- Salt
- Toppings: cheese, bacon, or sliced ham (all optional)

Preparation:

- Preheat your oven to 450°F (230°C).
- Flatten the ground meat on a baking sheet to form a "crust" and season with salt.
- Bake until the meat is cooked through, about 10 minutes.
- Add cheese and other toppings if desired and return to oven until cheese is melted. Serve.

---

14. Tuna Steak with Lemon Butter

Prep Time: 5 mins

Cook Time: 6 mins

Ingredients:

- 2 tuna steaks
- Salt
- Butter
- Lemon juice (optional)

Preparation:

- Season tuna steaks with salt.
- Heat butter in a skillet over medium-high heat until melted and frothy.
- Sear tuna for about 3 minutes per side.
- Drizzle with lemon juice if using and serve immediately.

---

15. Duck Breast A L'Orange

Prep Time: 10 mins

Cook Time: 15 mins

Ingredients:

- 2 duck breasts
- Salt
- Orange zest (optional, not for strict carnivore)

Preparation:

- Score the skin of the duck breasts and season with salt and orange zest if using.
- Cook skin side down in a cold skillet, then turn heat to medium-high.
- Cook until skin is crispy, flip and cook to desired doneness. Serve.

16. Bone Marrow on Toast

Prep Time: 5 mins

Cook Time: 20 mins

Ingredients:

- Beef marrow bones
- Salt
- Carnivore-friendly toast (optional)

Preparation:

- Preheat the oven to 450°F (230°C).
- Season the marrow bones with salt.
- Roast in the preheated oven until the marrow is soft and slightly bubbly.
- Scoop out the marrow and spread onto carnivore-friendly toast if desired. Serve.

17. Grilled Lamb Chops with Garlic Butter

Prep Time: 5 mins

Cook Time: 10 mins

Ingredients:

- 4 lamb chops
- Salt
- Garlic butter (optional)

Preparation:

- Season lamb chops with salt.
- Grill over high heat to your desired level of doneness.
- Top with a slice of garlic butter if desired and serve.

18. Carnivore Diet Omelette

Prep Time: 5 mins

Cook Time: 5 mins

Ingredients:

- 3 eggs

- Salt
- Butter
- Cheese (optional)

Preparation:

- Beat the eggs with a pinch of salt.
- Melt butter in a non-stick skillet and pour in the eggs.
- Cook gently, and add cheese if using before folding the omelette. Serve.

---

19. Bison Burger Patties

Prep Time: 5 mins

Cook Time: 10 mins

Ingredients:

- 1 lb ground bison
- Salt

Preparation:

- Form the bison into patties and season with salt.
- Cook in a skillet over medium-high heat to your preferred level of doneness.
- Serve alone or with a side of your favorite carnivore-approved toppings.

---

20. Carnivore Diet Bone Broth

Prep Time: 10 mins

Cook Time: 12-24 hrs

Ingredients:

- 2 lbs of mixed beef bones (marrow, knuckle, rib, etc.)
- Salt
- Water

Preparation:

- Preheat your oven to 400°F (200°C) and roast the bones for 30 minutes.
- Transfer the bones to a large pot or slow cooker and cover with water.
- Add a generous amount of salt.
- Bring to a simmer and cook on low for 12-24 hours, skimming off any impurities that rise to the top.

- Strain the broth and serve hot, or store for later use.

Dinner Recipes

1. Classic Ribeye Steak

Prep Time: 5 mins

Cook Time: 6-8 mins

Ingredients:

- 1 ribeye steak
- Salt

Preparation:

- Preheat your grill or skillet over high heat.
- Season the steak generously with salt.
- Cook the steak for 3-4 minutes on each side for medium-rare, or to your preferred level of doneness.
- Let it rest for a few minutes before serving.

---

2. Baked Pork Chops

Prep Time: 5 mins

Cook Time: 18-20 mins

Ingredients:

- 4 pork chops
- Salt

Preparation:

- Preheat your oven to 400°F (200°C).
- Season pork chops with salt.
- Bake in the preheated oven for 18-20 minutes or until internal temperature reaches 145°F (63°C).
- Let them rest before serving.

---

3. Lamb Loin Chops

Prep Time: 5 mins

Cook Time: 10-12 mins

Ingredients:

- 4 lamb loin chops
- Salt

Preparation:

- Season the lamb chops with salt.
- Heat a skillet over medium-high heat and cook the chops for 5-6 minutes on each side.
- Rest the chops for a few minutes before serving.

---

4. Seared Ahi Tuna Steaks

Prep Time: 5 mins

Cook Time: 4 mins

Ingredients:

- 2 ahi tuna steaks
- Salt

Preparation:

- Season the tuna steaks with salt.
- Sear the steaks in a hot skillet for 1-2 minutes per side.
- Serve immediately.

---

5. Grilled Chicken Thighs

Prep Time: 5 mins

Cook Time: 20 mins

Ingredients:

- 6 chicken thighs, skin on
- Salt

Preparation:

- Preheat grill to medium-high heat.
- Season chicken thighs with salt.
- Grill skin side down for 10 minutes, then flip and grill for another 10 minutes.
- Serve when the internal temperature reaches 165°F (74°C).

---

6. Pan-Fried Duck Breast

Prep Time: 10 mins

Cook Time: 15 mins

Ingredients:

- 2 duck breasts
- Salt

Preparation:

- Score the skin of the duck breast and season with salt.
- Place skin side down in a cold skillet and turn the heat to medium.
- Cook for about 10 minutes until the skin is crispy, then flip and cook for another 5 minutes.
- Rest before serving.

7. Broiled Lobster Tails

Prep Time: 5 mins

Cook Time: 10 mins

Ingredients:

- 2 lobster tails
- Salt

Preparation:

- Preheat the broiler.
- Split the lobster tails in half and season with salt.
- Broil for about 10 minutes or until the meat is opaque and cooked through.
- Serve immediately.

8. Grilled Veal Chops

Prep Time: 5 mins

Cook Time: 12 mins

Ingredients:

- 2 veal chops
- Salt

Preparation:

- Preheat the grill to high.
- Season the veal chops with salt.
- Grill for 6 minutes per side.
- Rest the chops before serving.

9. Roasted Quail

Prep Time: 10 mins

Cook Time: 20 mins

Ingredients:

- 4 quails
- Salt

Preparation:

- Preheat your oven to 450°F (230°C).
- Season the quails inside and out with salt.
- Roast in the oven for 20 minutes or until the internal temperature reaches 165°F (74°C).
- Let rest before serving.

10. Pan-Seared Scallops

Prep Time: 5 mins

Cook Time: 4 mins

Ingredients:

- 12 large sea scallops
- Salt

Preparation:

- Season the scallops with salt.
- Heat a skillet over high heat and add the scallops without overcrowding.
- Sear for 2 minutes on each side until a golden crust forms.
- Serve immediately.

11. Grilled Swordfish

Prep Time: 5 mins

Cook Time: 10 mins

Ingredients:

- 2 swordfish steaks
- Salt

Preparation:

- Preheat your grill to medium-high heat.
- Season the swordfish steaks with salt.
- Grill for about 5 minutes on each side until the fish flakes easily with a fork.
- Serve hot off the grill.

---

12. Bacon-Wrapped Filet Mignon

Prep Time: 10 mins

Cook Time: 12 mins

Ingredients:

- 2 filet mignon steaks
- 4 slices of bacon
- Salt

Preparation:

- Wrap each steak with 2 slices of bacon and secure with toothpicks.
- Season with salt.
- Preheat your skillet over medium-high heat.
- Cook the steaks to your preferred doneness, about 5-6 minutes per side for medium-rare.
- Let them rest before serving.

---

13. Venison Tenderloin

Prep Time: 5 mins

Cook Time: 10 mins

Ingredients:

- 1 venison tenderloin
- Salt

Preparation:

- Preheat your skillet or grill.

- Season the tenderloin with salt.

- Cook over high heat for 5 minutes on each side.

- Allow to rest, then slice against the grain before serving.

---

14. Grilled Shrimp Skewers

Prep Time: 10 mins

Cook Time: 6 mins

Ingredients:

- 16 large shrimp, peeled and deveined

- Salt

Preparation:

- Preheat grill to high.

- Season the shrimp with salt and thread onto skewers.

- Grill for 2-3 minutes per side until opaque and cooked through.

- Serve immediately.

---

15. Beef Heart Steak

Prep Time: 10 mins

Cook Time: 8 mins

Ingredients:

- 1 beef heart, sliced into steaks

- Salt

Preparation:

- Season the beef heart steaks with salt.

- Preheat a skillet over medium-high heat.

- Cook for 4 minutes per side.

- Let the steaks rest before serving.

---

16. Grilled Turkey Legs

Prep Time: 5 mins

Cook Time: 1 hr

Ingredients:

- 2 turkey legs
- Salt

Preparation:

- Preheat your grill to medium-low heat.
- Season the turkey legs with salt.
- Grill for about 1 hour, turning occasionally, until the internal temperature reaches 165°F (74°C).
- Serve the turkey legs once they are cooked through.

---

17. Seared Foie Gras

Prep Time: 10 mins

Cook Time: 4 mins

Ingredients:

- 4 slices of foie gras
- Salt

Preparation:

- Season the foie gras slices with salt.
- Sear in a very hot, dry skillet for about 1-2 minutes per side.
- Serve immediately on warm plates.

---

18. Roasted Bone Marrow

Prep Time: 5 mins

Cook Time: 20 mins

Ingredients:

- 4 beef marrow bones
- Salt

Preparation:

- Preheat oven to 450°F (230°C).
- Season marrow bones with salt.
- Roast in the oven until the marrow is soft and has begun to separate from the bone, about 20 minutes.

- Serve the marrow with a spoon for scooping.

---

19. Beef Liver and Onions

Prep Time: 10 mins

Cook Time: 10 mins

Ingredients:

- 1 beef liver, sliced
- 1 onion, thinly sliced (optional, omit for strict carnivore diet)
- Salt

Preparation:

- Season the liver slices with salt.
- Heat a skillet over medium-high heat and cook the liver for 3-4 minutes per side.
- If including onions, cook them in the same skillet

---

20. Pan-Seared Salmon

Prep Time: 5 mins

Cook Time: 8 mins

Ingredients:

- 2 salmon fillets
- Salt

Preparation:

- Season the salmon fillets with salt.
- Heat a non-stick skillet over medium-high heat.
- Place the salmon skin-side down and cook for about 5 minutes until the skin is crispy.
- Flip the salmon and cook for another 3 minutes or until desired doneness.
- Serve immediately.

Snack and Side Dish Ideas

1. Crispy Chicken Skins

Prep Time: 5 mins

Cook Time: 15 mins

Ingredients:

- Chicken skins from 4 thighs

Preparation:

- Preheat the oven to 375°F (190°C).
- Lay chicken skins flat on a baking sheet lined with parchment paper.
- Bake for 15 minutes or until crispy.
- Let cool and enjoy as a crunchy snack.

---

2. Pork Rinds

Prep Time: 5 mins

Cook Time: Varies by method

Ingredients:

- Pork skin

Preparation:

- Cut pork skin into bite-sized pieces.
- Dry them out in a dehydrator or oven at a low temperature until fully dried.
- Deep fry in lard or tallow until puffy and crisp.
- Season with salt and let cool before serving.

---

3. Beef Jerky

Prep Time: 10 mins (plus marinating time)

Cook Time: 3-4 hours

Ingredients:

- Sliced beef (lean cuts work best)
- Salt

Preparation:

- Season beef slices with salt.
- Lay the slices on a baking rack over a baking sheet.
- Place in an oven at its lowest setting with the door slightly open until dehydrated and jerky-like, about 3-4 hours.
- Cool and store in an airtight container.

---

4. Deviled Eggs

Prep Time: 10 mins

Cook Time: 12 mins

Ingredients:

- 6 eggs
- 2 tablespoons mayonnaise
- Salt

Preparation:

- Hard boil eggs, peel, and cut in half lengthwise.
- Remove yolks and mix with mayonnaise and a pinch of salt.
- Spoon or pipe the yolk mixture back into the egg whites.
- Serve as a snack or side.

---

5. Bacon Sticks

Prep Time: 5 mins

Cook Time: 15-20 mins

Ingredients:

- 8 strips of bacon

Preparation:

- Preheat oven to 400°F (200°C).
- Twist each bacon strip and lay on a baking sheet with parchment paper.
- Bake until crisp, about 15-20 minutes.
- Serve as a crunchy snack.

---

6. Carnivore Scotch Eggs

Prep Time: 10 mins

Cook Time: 20 mins

Ingredients:

- 4 eggs
- 1 pound ground sausage meat
- Salt

Preparation:

- Preheat oven to 400°F (200°C).
- Hard boil eggs, cool, peel, and set aside.
- Season sausage meat with salt and flatten into patties.
- Encase each egg in sausage meat and place on a baking sheet.
- Bake for 20 minutes or until the sausage is cooked through.
- Serve warm or cold.

---

7. Bone Broth

Prep Time: 10 mins

Cook Time: 12-24 hours

Ingredients:

- Bones from beef, chicken, or pork
- Salt
- Water

Preparation:

- Place bones in a large pot or slow cooker.
- Add salt and cover with water.
- Simmer on low for 12-24 hours.
- Strain the broth, cool, and sip as a warm, nourishing drink.

---

8. Carnivore Pancakes

Prep Time: 5 mins

Cook Time: 8 mins

Ingredients:

- 4 ounces cream cheese
- 4 eggs
- Salt

Preparation:

- Blend cream cheese, eggs, and a pinch of salt until smooth.
- Pour batter into a hot, non-stick pan to form small pancakes.

- Cook until golden brown on both sides.
- Serve immediately.

---

9. Liver Pâté

Prep Time: 10 mins

Cook Time: 5 mins

Ingredients:

- 1 pound chicken livers
- 1/2 cup butter
- Salt

Preparation:

- Clean the livers and sauté in butter until cooked through.
- Season with salt and blend untilsmooth.
- Chill the pâté in the fridge for a few hours before serving.

---

10. Egg Muffins

Prep Time: 5 mins

Cook Time: 15 mins

Ingredients:

- 6 eggs
- 1/2 cup cooked bacon or sausage
- Salt

Preparation:

- Preheat oven to 350°F (175°C).
- Whisk eggs with salt.
- Grease muffin tins and evenly distribute the cooked bacon or sausage among them.
- Pour the eggs over the meat in the muffin tins.
- Bake for 15 minutes or until the eggs are set.
- Let cool slightly before serving.

Carnivore Diet-Friendly Condiments and Seasonings

1. Beef Tallow Mayo

Prep Time: 10 mins

Ingredients:

- 1 egg yolk
- 1 cup beef tallow, melted and cooled
- Salt

Preparation:

- Place the egg yolk in a blender and start blending on low speed.
- Slowly drizzle in the cooled beef tallow until the mixture emulsifies and becomes thick.
- Season with salt to taste.
- Store in the refrigerator and use within a week.

---

2. Carnivore Butter Spread

Prep Time: 5 mins

Ingredients:

- 1 cup butter, softened
- Salt (optional)

Preparation:

- Whip the butter with a mixer until it's light and fluffy.
- Season with a pinch of salt if desired.
- Store in the refrigerator and use as a spread or to add flavor to cooked meats.

---

3. Bone Marrow Butter

Prep Time: 10 mins

Cook Time: 20 mins

Ingredients:

- 4 marrow bones
- 1 cup butter, softened
- Salt

Preparation:

- Roast marrow bones at 450°F (230°C) for 20 minutes.
- Scoop out the marrow and mix with softened butter.
- Season with salt to taste.
- Use immediately, or store in the refrigerator.

---

4. Carnivore BBQ Sauce

Prep Time: 5 mins

Cook Time: 10 mins

Ingredients:

- 1 cup rendered bacon fat
- 1 tablespoon apple cider vinegar (optional for strict carnivores)
- Salt

Preparation:

- Combine bacon fat and apple cider vinegar in a saucepan and warm over low heat.
- Season with salt to taste.
- Use as a dip or sauce for meats, keeping in mind that vinegar is not strictly carnivore.

---

5. Pemmican Paste

Prep Time: 15 mins

Ingredients:

- 1/2 cup rendered beef tallow
- 1/2 cup dried beef powder (beef jerky ground into a powder)

Preparation:

- Warm the tallow until it's liquid.
- Mix in the dried beef powder until well combined.
- Use as a spread or eat as is for a high-energy snack.

---

6. Egg Yolk Sauce

Prep Time: 5 mins

Ingredients:

- 2 egg yolks

- Salt

Preparation:

- Whisk the egg yolks with a fork until creamy.
- Season with salt to taste.
- Serve immediately over steaks or burgers.

---

7. Baconnaise

Prep Time: 10 mins

Ingredients:

- 1/2 cup bacon fat, cooled to room temperature
- 1 egg yolk
- Salt

Preparation:

- In a blender, combine the egg yolk and bacon fat.
- Blend until the mixture becomes emulsified and thickened.
- Season with salt to taste.
- Store in the refrigerator and use within a few days.

---

8. Carnivore Gravy

Prep Time: 5 mins

Cook Time: 10 mins

Ingredients:

- Drippings from cooked meat (beef, pork, or chicken)
- Salt
- 1 tsp gelatin powder (for thickening)

Preparation:

- Pour drippings into a saucepan and heat over medium heat.
- Sprinkle in the gelatin powder and whisk until dissolved and the gravy thickens.
- Season with salt to taste.
- Serve hot over meat dishes.

---

9. Liver Pâté Spread

Prep Time: 10 mins

Cook Time: 10 mins

Ingredients:

- 1/2 pound chicken livers
- 1/4 cup butter
- Salt

Preparation:

- Cook the chicken livers in butter until fully cooked.
- Blend the livers and cooking fat together until smooth.
- Season with salt to taste.
- Use as a spread or dip once cooled.

---

10. Carnivore Hollandaise Sauce

Prep Time: 5 mins

Cook Time: 10 mins

Ingredients:

- 3 egg yolks
- 1 cup butter, melted
- 1 tablespoon lemon juice (optional for strict carnivores)
- Salt

Preparation:

- Whisk egg yolks in a heatproof bowl until creamy.
- Place the bowl over a pot of simmering water (double boiler) and continue to whisk, being careful not to let the eggs scramble.
- Slowly drizzle in the melted butter while whisking vigorously until the sauce thickens.
- Remove from heat, and whisk in lemon juice if using. Season with salt to taste.
- Serve immediately with steak, eggs, or other meats.

Batch Cooking and Meal Prep Strategies

1. Slow-Cooked Beef Brisket

Prep Time: 10 mins

Cook Time: 8 hours

Ingredients:

- 5 lbs beef brisket
- Salt

Preparation:

- Season the beef brisket generously with salt.
- Place it in a slow cooker on low heat for 8 hours or until tender.
- Slice or shred for meals throughout the week.

---

2. Carnivore Meatballs

Prep Time: 15 mins

Cook Time: 25 mins

Ingredients:

- 2 lbs ground beef
- 2 eggs
- Salt

Preparation:

- Preheat your oven to 375°F (190°C).
- Mix ground beef, eggs, and salt together in a bowl.
- Form into meatballs and place on a baking sheet.
- Bake for 25 minutes or until cooked through.
- Store in the refrigerator and reheat for meals.

---

3. Baked Chicken Thighs

Prep Time: 5 mins

Cook Time: 40 mins

Ingredients:

- 10 chicken thighs
- Salt

Preparation:

- Preheat your oven to 400°F (200°C).

- Season chicken thighs with salt and place on a baking tray.
- Bake for 40 minutes or until the skin is crispy and the chicken is cooked through.
- Keep in the fridge and use as needed.

---

4. Boiled Eggs

Prep Time: 2 mins

Cook Time: 10 mins

Ingredients:

- 12 large eggs
- Water

Preparation:

- Place eggs in a large pot and cover with cold water.
- Bring to a boil, then cover and remove from heat.
- Let stand for 10 minutes, then transfer to an ice bath.
- Peel or store with the shell on for quick snacks or additions to meals.

---

5. Pork Shoulder Roast

Prep Time: 10 mins

Cook Time: 6 hours

Ingredients:

- 1 pork shoulder roast (about 5 lbs)
- Salt

Preparation:

- Season the pork shoulder with salt.
- Place in a roasting pan and cook in the oven at 250°F (120°C) for about 6 hours or until it falls apart easily.
- Shred the pork and store for various meals, like pulled pork plates.

---

6. Carnivore Chili

Prep Time: 15 mins

Cook Time: 2 hours

Ingredients:

- 3 lbs ground beef
- 1 lb bacon, chopped
- Salt
- Water (as needed)

Preparation:

- Brown the ground beef and bacon in a large pot over medium heat.
- Once cooked, drain excess fat if desired.
- Add water just to cover the meat and bring to a simmer.
- Let cook on low heat for about 2 hours until you get a thick chili-like consistency.
- Cool and store in portions.

---

7. Ribeye Steaks

Prep Time: 5 mins

Cook Time: 10 mins

Ingredients:

- 4 ribeye steaks
- Salt

Preparation:

- Preheat your grill or skillet to high heat.
- Season the ribeye steaks with salt.
- Cook for about 5 minutes per side for medium-rare, or to your preferred doneness.
- Let rest, then store in the fridge to eat throughout the week.

---

8. Baked Salmon Fillets

Prep Time: 5 mins

Cook Time: 15 mins

Ingredients:

- 4 salmon fillets
- Salt

Preparation:

- Preheat your oven to 400°F (200°C).

- Season the salmon fillets with salt and place on a lined baking sheet.

- Bake for about 15 minutes or until cooked through.

- Cool and store in the refrigerator.

---

9. Carnivore Pancakes

Prep Time: 10 mins

Cook Time: 15 mins

Ingredients:

- 8 oz cream cheese

- 8 eggs

- Salt

Preparation:

- Blend cream cheese, eggs, and a pinch of salt in a food processor until smooth.

- Preheat a non-stick skillet over medium-low heat.

- Pour batter to form small pancakes and cook until golden on each side.

- Cool and store in the refrigerator, reheat in a skillet when ready to eat.

---

10. Liver and Onions

Prep Time: 10 mins

Cook Time: 15 mins

Ingredients:

- 2 lbs beef liver, sliced

- 1 lb bacon

- Salt

Preparation:

- Cook bacon in a large skillet until crispy. Set bacon aside and leave the fat in the skillet.

- Season liver slices with salt and sear in the bacon fat over medium-high heat for about 2 minutes per side or until cooked to your liking.

- Store liver and bacon together in containers.

- Reheat gently to maintain the tenderness of the liver.

Carnivore Diet Recipes for Special Occasions and Holidays

1. Roast Leg of Lamb

Prep Time: 20 mins

Cook Time: 2 hours

Ingredients:

- 1 whole leg of lamb (around 5-7 lbs)
- Salt
- Fresh rosemary (optional, for those who allow herbs on their carnivore diet)

Preparation:

- Preheat your oven to 350°F (175°C).
- Season the leg of lamb generously with salt and rosemary.
- Roast in the oven for about 2 hours, or until the internal temperature reaches 145°F (63°C) for medium-rare.
- Let the lamb rest for 15-20 minutes before carving.

---

2. Beef Wellington (Carnivore Style)

Prep Time: 30 mins

Cook Time: 45 mins

Ingredients:

- 2.5 lbs beef tenderloin
- Salt
- 2 lbs ground pork
- 1 egg (for egg wash)

Preparation:

- Preheat your oven to 400°F (200°C).
- Season the beef tenderloin with salt and sear on all sides in a hot skillet.
- Spread ground pork over a layer of cling film to the size of the tenderloin.
- Wrap the seared tenderloin in the ground pork.
- Brush with egg wash and bake for 45 minutes, or until the internal temperature reaches 130°F (54°C) for medium-rare.
- Let it rest before slicing.

---

3. Prime Rib Roast

Prep Time: 10 mins

Cook Time: 2 hours

Ingredients:

- 1 prime rib roast (about 5 lbs)
- Salt

Preparation:

- Preheat your oven to 500°F (260°C).
- Season the prime rib roast liberally with salt.
- Roast for about 5 minutes per pound for a perfect crust.
- Turn off the oven and let the roast sit inside for 2 hours without opening the door.
- Remove the roast and let it rest for at least 15 minutes before carving.

---

4. Surf and Turf

Prep Time: 10 mins

Cook Time: 15 mins

Ingredients:

- 2 lobster tails
- 2 fillet mignon steaks
- Salt
- Butter (optional, if dairy is permitted in your version of the carnivore diet)

Preparation:

- Preheat your grill or skillet to high heat for the steaks and preheat your oven to 350°F (175°C) for the lobster tails.
- Season steaks with salt and cook to your preferred doneness, typically 3-4 minutes per side for medium-rare.
- Split lobster tails down the middle, season with salt, and place a dollop of butter on top if using.
- Bake lobster tails for about 12-15 minutes or until fully cooked.
- Serve the steak and lobster tail together for a luxurious meal.

---

5. Whole Roasted Turkey

Prep Time: 20 mins

Cook Time: 3 hours

Ingredients:

- 1 whole turkey (about 12-14 lbs)
- Salt

Preparation:

- Preheat your oven to 325°F (165°C).
- Pat the turkey dry and season inside and out with salt.
- Place the turkey on a rack in a roasting pan and cover loosely with aluminum foil.
- Roast for about 3 hours or until the internal temperature reaches 165°F (74°C) in the thickest part of the thigh.
- Remove the foil in the last 30 minutes to brown the skin.
- Let the turkey rest before carving.

---

6. Pork Crown Roast

Prep Time: 20 mins

Cook Time: 2 hours 30 mins

Ingredients:

- 1 pork crown roast (12-14 ribs)
- Salt

Preparation:

- Preheat your oven to 350°F (175°C).
- Season the pork crown roast thoroughly with salt.
- Place the roast in a large roasting pan and cook for about 2 hours and 30 minutes, or until the internal temperature reaches 145°F (63°C).
- Let it rest for at least 20 minutes before slicing between the rib bonesand serving.

---

7. Carnivore Diet Christmas Ham

Prep Time: 15 mins

Cook Time: 2 hours

Ingredients:

- 1 bone-in ham (8-10 lbs)
- Salt

Preparation:

- Preheat your oven to 325°F (165°C).
- Score the ham's surface with shallow cuts and season with salt.
- Place the ham in a roasting pan and bake for approximately 2 hours, or until the internal temperature reaches 140°F (60°C).
- Let the ham rest for 15-20 minutes before slicing.

---

8. New Year's Eve Ribeye Steaks

Prep Time: 5 mins

Cook Time: 10 mins

Ingredients:

- 2 ribeye steaks, 1-inch thick
- Salt

Preparation:

- Let the steaks come to room temperature for about 30 minutes.
- Preheat your grill or skillet to high heat.
- Season the steaks liberally with salt.
- Grill each side for about 4-5 minutes for medium-rare.
- Let the steaks rest for 5-10 minutes before serving.

---

9. Easter Roast Chicken

Prep Time: 10 mins

Cook Time: 1 hour 30 mins

Ingredients:

- 1 whole chicken (4-5 lbs)
- Salt

Preparation:

- Preheat your oven to 425°F (220°C).
- Pat the chicken dry and season it inside and out with salt.
- Place the chicken breast-side up in a roasting pan and roast for about 1 hour and 30 minutes, or until the internal temperature reaches 165°F (74°C) in the thickest part of the thigh.
- Let the chicken rest for 10 minutes before carving.

10. Grilled Rack of Pork Ribs (4th of July Special)

Prep Time: 10 mins

Cook Time: 1 hour 30 mins

Ingredients:

- 1 rack of pork ribs
- Salt

Preparation:

- Preheat your grill to 300°F (150°C) for indirect grilling.
- Season the ribs all over with salt.
- Place ribs on the indirect heat side of the grill and cook for about 1.5 hours or until the meat is tender and pulls away from the bones.
- Optionally, finish over direct heat for a few minutes to get a crispy exterior.
- Let the ribs rest for 10 minutes before cutting into individual ribs and serving.

Carnivore Diet Recipes for Travel and On-the-Go

1. Beef Jerky

Prep Time: 10 mins

Marinating Time: 8 hours

Dehydrating Time: 4-8 hours

Ingredients:

- 2 lbs lean beef, sliced thinly
- Salt

Preparation:

- Season the beef slices generously with salt.
- Lay the slices on a dehydrator tray without overlapping.
- Dehydrate at 160°F (71°C) for 4-8 hours, depending on thickness, until fully dried.
- Store in an airtight container and enjoy as a portable snack.

2. Hard-Boiled Eggs

Prep Time: 1 min

Cook Time: 9-12 mins

Ingredients:

- 6 large eggs

Preparation:

- Place eggs in a pot and cover with water.
- Bring to a boil, then cover and remove from heat.
- Let stand for 9-12 minutes for hard-boiled eggs.
- Cool in ice water, peel, and pack for a quick, portable snack.

3. Canned Sardines

Prep Time: 1 min

Ingredients:

- 1 can of sardines in water or olive oil

Preparation:

- Simply pack the can with you, and when you're ready to eat, open it and enjoy.

4. Pork Rinds

Prep Time: 5 mins

Cook Time: 10 mins

Ingredients:

- Pork skin, cut into bite-sized pieces

Preparation:

- Place the pork skin pieces in a microwave-safe dish.
- Microwave on high for 2-3 minutes or until they puff up and are crispy.
- Let them cool and pack them in a sealable bag.

5. Smoked Salmon Roll-Ups

Prep Time: 5 mins

Ingredients:

- Smoked salmon slices
- Cream cheese (optional, if dairy is permitted)

Preparation:

- Spread cream cheese on smoked salmon slices if using.
- Roll up the slices and pack them in a container for a portable snack.

---

6. Cold-Cut Meats and Cheese

Prep Time: 5 mins

Ingredients:

- Assorted cold cuts (e.g., ham, turkey, roast beef)
- Slices of cheese (optional)

Preparation:

- Layer cold cuts with cheese slices, roll them up, and pack in a container.

---

7. Bacon Strips

Prep Time: 2 mins

Cook Time: 10-20 mins

Ingredients:

- Thick-cut bacon strips

Preparation:

- Lay bacon strips on a baking sheet.
- Bake at 400°F (200°C) for 10-20 minutes until crispy.
- Cool and pack in a sealable bag for a crunchy snack.

---

8. Chicken Drumsticks

Prep Time: 5 mins

Cook Time: 45 mins

Ingredients:

- Chicken drumsticks
- Salt

Preparation:

- Season drumsticks with salt.
- Bake at 375°F (190°C) for 45 minutes, or until cooked through.
- Cool and pack for a portable meal.

9. Tuna Pouches

Prep Time: 1 min

Ingredients:

- 1 pouch of tuna in water

Preparation:

- Pack the sealed pouch and simply open it when you're ready to eat.

10. Cooked Shrimp

Prep Time: 5 mins

Cook Time: 3 mins

Ingredients:

- Shrimp, peeled and deveined

Preparation:

- Boil shrimp for 2-3 minutes until pink and opaque.
- Cool and pack in a container for a refreshing, high-protein snack.

3 BONUS EBOOKS

Scan the QR CODE and receive the 3 bonus ebooks

Ayurveda Cooking for Beginners

Chinese Takeout Cookbook

The Pizza Bible

http://subscribepage.io/01tYl3

Amanda Quinn

Made in the USA
Monee, IL
30 June 2024

60960571R00059